To Be Human: Accounts Vary Widely

# To Be Human: Accounts Vary Widely

Dan Williams

Copyright 2024 @ Dan Williams
All Rights Reserved

ISBN: 978-1-962148-17-7
LOC: 2025934072
Editor: Mikaela Bartlett
Cover Design: Jerry Craven
Photographs: Dan Williams

Lamar University Literary Press
Beaumont, TX

# Acknowledgements

Many thanks to the editor of the following anthology for publishing some of the poems (or earlier versions of them) in this book:

*Writing Texas*, Vol. 10, edited by John Schulze

Five of the poems that appear in these pages were previously published in the annual TACWT publication, *Writing Texas*, Vol. 10, edited by John Schulze: "What the Aztecs Believed," "Henry VIII Foully Imbued," "Frederick the Great Not So Great," "Cicero's Six Mistakes Mankind Keeps Making Century After Century," and "Lake Worth, Despite the Din."

# Acknowledging Friends and Influences

*"Gratitude is not only the greatest of virtues, but the parent of all the others. Gratitude makes sense of our past, brings peace for today, and creates hope for tomorrow."*
    —Cicero

When he was writing *Walden,* Thoreau remarked that he stopped reading because he did not want his words to be influenced by other writers. But Thoreau was mistaken to think he could shut off the influence of others. No one writes in a vacuum.

Jerry Craven has been a constant friend, guide, editor, and supporter. His influence has been tremendous, and I am most grateful. I am also grateful for Larry Mayfield, a good friend and a fine poet, who astutely commented on my poems. I have been inspired by two excellent poets who recently passed, Walt McDonald and Jim Hoggard, and I have been equally inspired by so many outstanding TACWT writers. Each year at the annual TACWT meeting I am amazed at the quality of their writing.

My colleagues here at TCU have been equally inspirational and supportive. I am immensely thankful for the people I work with at TCU Press, Tameko, Adrienne, Marco, and James, for my colleagues in Honors, and for those remarkable friends who have not only helped me but who have graciously supported TCU Press. Thank you Mark, Leo, Michael, Rich, Adam, Newell, Caroline, Peggy, and Jeff. I humbly acknowledge your influences. I am also most grateful for TCU. I arrived over two decades ago, a refugee from an impoverished state school, and I found a welcome and a home. I am particularly indebted to Chancellor Victor Boschini, under whose leadership and support I have thrived.

With great appreciation I also acknowledge the help I have received from Lamar University Literary Press, which in a mere decade has established itself as one of the primary promoters of Texas literary culture. Lamar's list of writers and books represent some of the best writing in Texas. For this book, I especially am thankful for Mikaela Bartlett, who edited this collection. Her help has been immeasurable.

Finally, with profound appreciation, I express my thanks to Cynthia and Leah, wife and daughter. In every book I have ever published I have referred to them as the pillars of my life, and so they remain.

This book is dedicated to Bob Frye, Ron Moore, Paul Boller, and Barry Hannah, four great friends who trusted me with their friendship. Though they are no longer here, their spirits and memories remain inspirational and consoling.

# Recent Poetry from Lamar University Literary Press

Lisa Adams, *Xuai*
Walter Bargen, *Radiation Diary: Return to the Sea*
Christine Boldt, *In Every Tatter*
Devan Burton, *A Room for Us*
Jerry Bradley, *Collapsing into Possibility*
Mark Busby, *Through Our Times*
Julie Chappell, *Mad Habits of a Life*
Stan Crawford, *Resisting Gravity*
Glover Davis, *Academy of Dreams*
Wendy Dunmeyer, *My Grandmother's Last Letter*
Chris Ellery, *Elder Tree*
Kelly Ann Ellis, *The Hungry Ghost Diner*
Dede Fox, *On Wings of Silence*
Alan Gann, *That's Entertainment*
Larry Griffin, *Cedar Plums*
Lynn Hoggard, *First Light*
Michael Jennings, *Crossings: A Record of Travel*
Markham Johnson, *Dear Dreamland*
Betsy Joseph & Chip Dameron, *Relatively Speaking*
Jim McGarrah, *A Balancing Act*
J. Pittman McGehee, *Nod of Knowing*
David Meischen, *Caliche Road Poems*
Laurence Musgrove, *A Stranger's Heart*
Benjamin Myers, *The Family Book of Martyrs*
Janice Northerns, *Some Electric Hum*
Godspower Oboido, *Wandering Feet on Pebbled Shores*
Dave Oliphant, *Summing Up: Selected Poems*
Nathaniel O'Reilly, *Landmarks*
Carol Coffee Reposa, *Sailing West*
Steven Schroeder, *the moon, not the finger, pointing*
C.W. Smith, *The Museum of Marriage*
Vincent Spina, *The Sumptuous Hills of Gulfport*
W.K. Stratton, *Betrayal Creek*
Ken Waldman, *Sports Page*
Loretta Diane Walker, *Ode to My Mother's Voice*
Dan Williams, *At the Gates, a Refuge of Milkweed and Sunflowers*
Jonas Zdanys, *The Angled Road*

For information on these and other Lamar University Literary Press books go to www.Lamar.edu/literarypress

# Contents

|     |     |
| --- | --- |
| I.  | Preface: What Life Is All About |
| 13  | Dostoyevsky, After His Death Sentence Had Been Reprieved |
| 14  | Cicero's *Six Mistakes Mankind Keeps Making Century After Century* |
| 17  | What The Old Prophet Said |
| 18  | Homage to An Old Prophet: A Found Poem |
| 19  | After One Hundred Sunrises on Lake Worth |
| 20  | Lake Worth, Despite the Din |
| 21  | The Indifference of Swallows at Dawn |
| 22  | Caddo Sounds |
| 23  | The Still Before The Storm |
| 24  | A Sunny Wintry Afternoon |
|     |     |
| II. | Delectable Detriment |
|     |     |
| 27  | The Trial of Helena Scheuberin—And the Inquisitor's Revenge |
| 28  | Lines Taken From *Malleus Maleficarum* (1487): The Second Bestselling Book for Two Centuries |
| 30  | Lilith: Lady Flying in Darkness |
| 32  | Monstrous Females |
| 34  | The Kelpie |
| 35  | Succubi Still Exist |
| 37  | A French Pope And His Demon Lover |
| 39  | Dame Alice Kyteler, Ireland's First Condemned Witch |
| 41  | Isobel Gowdie's Four Confessions: Spokin and Willinglie Confest in 1662 |
| 43  | Never A Normal Life: Mother Shipton, A Sybil in North Yorkshire |
| 44  | Mary Lee, Bound for a New Land |
|     |     |
| III.| There Are Three Deaths |
|     |     |
| 49  | What the Aztecs Believed |
| 51  | Dancing with the Dead |
| 53  | The Devil's Pitchfork |
| 55  | Hermes Trismegistus, The Most Famous Man Alive Who Never Lived |
| 57  | John Gee, The Queen Called Him "My Philosopher" |
| 58  | Matthew Hopkins, Witch Finder General |
| 60  | Aleister Crowley, The Wickedest Man in the World |

| IV. | Indecent Exhibitions |
|---|---|
| 65 | Empress Theodora, The Most Powerful Woman in Byzantium |
| 68 | The Hippodrome of Constantinople |
| 69 | Something More Than I Was: Margot of Valois, Queen of France |
| 71 | The Saint Bartholomew's Day Massacre: "The Worst of the Century's Religious Massacres" |
| 74 | Madame de Pompadour: The Most Powerful Woman in France |
| 76 | Henry VIII Foully Imbued |
| 77 | Frederick the Great Not so Great |
| V. | Be Sure You're Right |
| 81 | Hell, According to Jonathan Edwards |
| 82 | Mamachtaga's Smile |
| 85 | "Be Sure You're Right Then Go Ahead": David Not Davy Crockett |
| 88 | Novel Reading, A Cause of Female Depravity: Lines Taken from *The Monthly Mirror,* November, 1797 |
| 90 | "The Poison They Infuse": Lines Taken from "The Ladies Department" in the *Zion's Herald*, December, 1825 |
| 91 | "The Good Wife": Lines Taken from *The Dawn*, May, 1822 |
| 92 | "To Rob Sweet Innocence Of Its All": Lines Taken from *The Ladies' Visitor*, February, 1820 |
| 94 | Make Belief, The Great American Invention |
| 96 | Victor "The Count" Lustig, The Smoothest Con Man that Ever Lived |
| 99 | If You Believe This . . . George C. Parker and the Brooklyn Bridge |
| 101 | The White Slavery Conspiracy: The Greatest Crime In the World's History |
| VI. | Epilogue: Great Values on Prehistoric Artifacts |
| 105 | A Weird Word, Wild |
| 106 | Archaeopteryx, The Feathered Lizard |
| 108 | Tracking Dinosaurs: Darwinism, Creationism, and Capitalism in the Muck of Time |

I. Preface: What Life Is All About

# Dostoyevsky, After His Death Sentence Had Been Reprieved

Sentenced to death for antigovernment
activities, for radical thought, Dostoevsky
was led before a firing squad, a cold morning
in December, a few days before Christmas,
but he was reprieved at the last moment
and sentenced to four years in a Siberian
labor camp—when thinking about life,
the being and not being, the inconstancy
and uncertainty, the volatility, the cruelty,
he remarked on the meaning of human
existence: "to be a human being among
people and to remain one forever, no
matter what circumstances, not to grow
despondent and not to lose heart—that is
what life is all about, that is its task."

# Cicero's *Six Mistakes Mankind Keeps Making Century After Century*

I
*Believing that personal*
*gain is made*
*by crushing others*

II
*Worrying about things*
*that cannot be changed*
*or corrected*

III
*Insisting that a thing*
*is impossible because*
*we cannot accomplish it*

IV
*Refusing to set aside*
*trivial preferences*

V
*Neglecting development*
*and refinement*
*of the mind*

VI
*Attempting to compel*
*others to believe*
*and live as we do*


Engels called him "the most
contemptible scoundrel
in history," hostile gangs

dogged him in Roman streets,
hurling abuse, stones, feces—
fearing his influence,

Marc Antony condemned him
as an enemy of the state,
and viciously pursued him,

when captured, Cicero bowed
to his captors, "I go no
further . . . sever this neck,"

his severed head and hands
were brought to Rome, Fulvia,
Antony's wife, in revenge

for his oratorical skill, pulled
out his tongue and jabbed
it with her hairpin,

head and hands were nailed
on the Rostra in the Roman
Forum, where he once spoke,

statesman, scholar, lawyer,
and philosopher, and one
of the greatest of all orators,

his influence is immense,
Petrarch rediscovered his
letters, which helped

to launch the Renaissance,
Erasmus, Martin Luther, and
John Locke admired him, his

*De Officiis* was the second
book Gutenberg printed,
after his Bible, Henry VIII

inscribed his copy, "thys
boke is myne Prynce Henry,"
Gibbon, Diderot, Hume, Voltaire,

and Montesquieu praised him,
as did Burke, John Adams, Jefferson,
and so many revolutionaries

devoted to human rights,
declared a righteous pagan
by the early church fathers,

Dante placed him in limbo,
merciful space for heathens,
his name means chickpea,

perhaps cultivated by his family,
or perhaps a common-sounding
name he chose as he shunned

pretension, he invented philosophy's
vocabulary, evidentia, humanitas,
qualitas, quantitas, and essential,

one of the greatest influences
on politics and philosophy, his
principles the bedrock of liberty.

# What The Old Prophet Said

The old prophet said words were signs,
symbols and glyphs scratched in rock
before rock, images of thought before
thought, ciphers of natural facts before
nature or facts, a world of wonder before
words were uttered, signifiers cleaving
light from dark in an old book existing
before books, poetry written before
writing, nature the symbol of spirit.

# Homage to An Old Prophet: A Found Poem

Wherever snow falls, or water flows,
or birds fly, wherever day and night
meet in twilight, wherever blue heaven
is hung by clouds, sown with stars,
wherever are forms with transparent
boundaries, wherever are outlets
into celestial space, wherever is danger,
and awe, and love, there is Beauty,
plenteous as rain, shed for thee,
and though thou shouldest walk
the world over, thou shalt not be able
to find a condition inopportune or ignoble.

# After One Hundred Sunrises on Lake Worth

*"This is a wonderful day. I have never seen one like this before."*
    —Maya Angelou

Each dawn's different, the same yet never
the same, nature's never static, a perpetual
pulse of water, wind, and weather, currents
and crosscurrents, each breeze ripples
across the lake, and new visions appear,

even on those motionless mirror-glass
mornings when earth and sky merge
and up becomes down, dawn's stillness
is never still, its silence never silent,
gulls rise and swirl before first light,

and in the woods birds begin to sing,
there's an infinite flow, high to low and low
to high, the same launch, the same lights
on the distant highway, the same circuit
around Goat Island always bring new views,

new breath, new wonders, new awe, each
sunrise a new dance of color and clouds,
each season, each day, kindles new reverie
and reverence, to glide among the reeds
and shallows, to listen to the words of wind

and water, a quiet oration, gives glimpses
of a world vaster than we presume—each
day's gift shames yet sustains, once an old
prophet preached that to perceive life's
fullness, we must think like a lake.

# Lake Worth, Despite the Din

Despite the din and drone of highway, the clusters
of houses and docks, the high rises rising above
the bridge, the human sprawl beyond, there's
persistence out on the water, a world of reed
and mud bank perseveres, a world too shallow
for watercraft, the bass boats and jet skis, where
mallards and cormorants gather, and egrets

and herons hunt, hugging the quiet shoreline,
undeterred by the detritus of human waste,
the plastic bottles and beer cans, the margin
between lake and city, to slip into these liminal
spaces, these quiet areas—an infinite spectrum
of color and current, of shade and sunlight,
of limitless sequence and succession—humbles,

there's privilege and promise when watching kingfishers
fish, hovering, suddenly darting, or a pair of ospreys
circling in the updrafts, and perchance, perched high
on a branch, an eagle watching for a glint of silver
below, the Great Blues and the Great Whites remain
skittish at human approach, too great the residual
memory of shotgun pellets, but sometimes a slow,

silent paddle allows a closer glimpse, and the fierce
eyes watch, ready to take flight and squawk at human
disturbance, to be acquainted with that marginal
world where deer and racoons appear at dawn, where
redwings and blackbirds greet the first touches of light,
that first touch of warmth, to congregate among
the birds, requires devotion, praise and prayer.

# The Indifference of Swallows at Dawn

Over the lake,
the boundless swallows
swiftly skim, dip, dart,
and circle, rising
and falling, chattering
in an ancient dialect,
they remain indifferent
to human commotion,
the incessant noise
of humans waking,
the grinding gears up
the hill, the buzzing
 of lawn mowers and leaf
blowers, they remain
distant and detached
and will persist until
the world's adjourned.

## Caddo Sounds

At night there's constant chatter,
the whir and chitter of insects,
thousands of crickets courting
and calling, and the katydid song
of grasshoppers, cicadas vibrating,
attracting, and thousands of frogs
and peepers croaking, announcing,
an endless concert of worlds beyond.

Before light birds begin singing,
filling the dark with the promise
of light, a new day, an infinite
chorus of trills, chirps, whistles,
warbles, tweets, and twitters,
songs and calls marking territory,
coaxing mates, signaling threats,

Caddo's a limitless labyrinth
of shallows and channels,
of Cypress trees and Spanish
moss, except for the whine
of motorboats, its silence
is pervasive, yet it's filled
with sound, a quiet defined
by what is heard and not heard,
the absence of interruption.

# The Still Before the Storm

Before the storm,
the lake is hushed
and still in morning
calm, sky and water
coalesce, and the boat
floats on clouds, around
a bend a heron takes
flight, a gray shape
flapping in cold mist,
rains are predicted,
the lake has not heard
the forecast, yet its stillness
speaks of storm.

# Winter Sun Near Twilight

A sunny wintry afternoon,
near twilight, the tallest trees
grasp the last glint of gold,
the hint of another day,
nearby bushes rustle
with birds roosting before
the dark and cold, there's
a calm acquiescence
as the sun recedes.

II.  A Desirable Calamity, A Domestic Danger, A Delectable Detriment

# The Trial of Helena Scheuberin—
# And The Inquisitor's Revenge

A likely target, she was independent, outspoken,
assertive, and aware of the rumors, the insinuations
of intrigues, she attacked, accusing the accuser,
confronting the Inquisitor publicly, she spat at him,
cursing, "Fie on you, you bad monk, may the falling
evil take you," disrupting his sermon she proclaimed
him an evil man in league with devils, his doctrines

heretical, she a young woman married to a prosperous
burger—the offended Inquisitor, aghast at her insults,
her perverse inversions of decorum, named her a witch,
her slanders proof of her perversions—in 1487, an October
morning near All Hallow's Eve, the trial began, Innsbruck
dignitaries, sacred and secular, gathered in the townhall
to witness the Inquisition, but from the start, the trial

went wild, ignoring the charges, the Inquisitor interrogated
her sexual history, asserting "all witches have been slaves
from a young age to carnal lust," claiming female sexuality
caused witchcraft, he accused her of having sex with devils,
the depravity of demonolatry, of burning with lust to satisfy
infernal, insatiable desires—alarmed by the indelicate inquiry
the Bishop's man requested he stop, but he continued

to offend, and the commissioners stopped the trial, soon
the Bishop, questioning the Inquisitor's sanity, expelled
him from the diocese, yet the Dominican had the last word,
literally—to take revenge, and promote misogyny, he soon
published *Malleus Maleficarum*, The Hammer of Witches,
an odious book that melded sorcery and heresy, that accused
all women of defects and deceit, that recommended torture

and deception to force confessions, that declared all witches
performed "filthy carnal acts with demons," that perceived
any female impropriety, even the slightest immodesty, a bare
ankle or arm, as evil incarnate, that without the slightest
hesitation quoted Exodus, "Thou shalt not suffer a witch
to live," and that burned witches for over two hundred
years, becoming the second most popular book in Europe.

# Lines Taken from *Malleus Maleficarum* (1487): The Second Bestselling Book for Two Centuries

I.     Concerning Devils:
They are unclean spirits . . . there is in them a natural madness, a rabid concupiscence, a wanton fancy . . . they are the enemies of the human race . . . subtle in wickedness, eager to hurt, ever fertile in fresh deceptions . . . they befoul the emotions of men . . . they bring diseases, stir up tempests, disguise themselves as angels of light, bear Hell always about them . . . always they lie in wait for the destruction of men; they have

a thousand ways of doing harm . . . to subvert and perturb the human race; yet their power remains confined to the privy parts . . . through the wantonness of the flesh they have much power over men; and in men the source of wantonness lies in the privy parts, since it is from them that semen falls, just as in women it falls from the naval . . . Satyrs and Fauns (and Incubi) have appeared to wanton women and . . . obtained coition.

II.    Concerning Witches:
Why is it that Women are chiefly addicted to Evil? this kind of perfidy is found more in the fragile sex than men; a woman knows no moderation; all wickedness is but little to the wickedness of a woman; what else is a woman but a foe to friendship, an unescapable punishment, a necessary evil, a natural temptation, a desirable calamity, a domestic danger, a delectable detriment, an evil of nature, painted with fair colors? The many lusts of men

lead them into one sin, but the lust of women leads them into all sins, for the root of all women's vices is avarice; superstition is chiefly found in Women; when a women thinks alone, she thinks evil; the word woman is used to mean lust of the flesh; women are intellectually like children; since they are feebler both in mind and body, it is not surprising that they should come more under the spell of witchcraft;

But the natural reason is that she is more carnal than men, as is clear from her many carnal abominations; when a woman weeps, she weaves snares . . . she labors to deceive; a wicked woman is by her nature quicker to waver in her faith . . . which is the root of witchcraft; no might of the flames or swollen winds

no deadly weapon, is so much to be feared as the lust and hatred
of a woman who has been divorced from the marriage bed;

adulterous drabs and whores are chiefly given to witchcraft;
on account of the blackness of their guilt . . . they distract
the minds of men, driving them to madness, insane hatred,
and inordinate lusts; incubi . . . lust lecherously after women,
and copulate with them; Witches may work some Prestidigatory
Illusion so that the Male Organ appears to be entirely removed;
witches can do marvelous things with regard to male organs;

Witches that are Midwives . . . Offer New-born Children
to Devils; the crimes of witches exceed . . . in guilt, in pain,
and in loss, all the evils which God allows; their deeds are more
evil than those of any other malefactors . . . Lucifer . . . has caused
a certain unusual heretical perversity to grow up in the land
of the Lord—a Heresy . . . of Sorceresses; the authors of *Malleus
Maleficarum* . . . toil to exterminate the sorceresses.

# Lilith: Lady Flying in Darkness

She had and has tons of names and titles, first woman, first
feminist, first wife of Adam, wife of Samael, Satan, and/or
Asmodeus, mother of demons—succubi, incubi, vampires,
lamia— mother of deceit, hot fiery female, primordial she-
demon, female night demon, bird-footed woman, night bird,

night creature, night hag, night monster, night owl, in King James
she's a screech owl, she's an unclean animal, dominant female,
incarnation of lust, Woman of Harlotry, temptress, witch, disease-
bearing wind spirit, bringer of death, killer of newborns, divine
feminine, Queen of Demons, Supreme Empress of Hell, Great

Goddess, Dark Lady, First Lady of Hell, Lilitu, perhaps Lolita, all
Lilith, the first woman. Tons of people worship her, Satanists,
Neo-Paganists, Wiccans, Druids, self-identified witches, in tons
of texts she appears, from the most ancient scrolls to the most
recent novels, poems, plays, films, TV shows, music, art, computer

games, anime, and manga, her stories continue to grow, endlessly
she's described and discussed, and she's even quoted in online
fandom sites like *The Demonic Paradise Wiki*, which recites: "I'm not
a man. I have no male pride for you to trick me with, and I
am not interested in single combat. That is entirely a weakness

of your sex, not mine. I am a woman. I will use any weapon and all
weapons to get what I want." One witch writer wrote: "No spirit exerts
more fascination over media and popular culture than Lilith. Her
appearances are genuinely too numerous to count." Over eons
her stories evolved, first in cuneiform tablets, and later in medieval

Hebrew texts as Adam's first wife, but Eden was never her paradise,
and she rebelled—made from the same clay on the same day as Adam,
Lilith believed she was his equal and refused female subservience, they
bickered about the sex thing, who's on top, the *Alphabet of Ben Sira*, a
satirical, heretical text, documents their quarrel, Lilith declares:

"I will not lie below," but Adam countered: "I will not lie below, but
above, since you are fit only for being below and I fit for being above."
Refusing to be below Adam, Lilith uttered "God's ineffable name

and flew away"—distraught at her desertion, Adam complained
to God: "Master of the Universe, the woman you gave me fled from

me"—rabbinic legends loosely concur she mated with Samael,
angel of death, together they bore hordes of Lilim, unclean children,
a 13th century text, the *Treatise of the Left Emanation*, imagines her
demon lovers merged to become Satan—other esoteric texts claim
God—to prevent their swarm from infesting the world—castrated

Samael, and Lilith, unable to control her lust, started assaulting men
at night, the Zohar text states: "She roams at night, and goes all about
the world and makes sport with men and causes them to emit seed."
Various Hebrew traditions aver she consorted with Asmodeus,
Prince of Hell, Prince of Lechery, and together they reigned in Sheol,

breeding scores of fiends, other sources relate she was lodged
in the Great Abyss until God called her to join Adam in Eden but she
she flew to the Cities of the Sea instead to attack humankind—still
others avow she loved and hated both Adam and Eve, and she returned
to Paradise and seduced them to impel humanity's corruption— so many

stories, so many sources, the stuff of dreams, male fears of female
fearlessness—at night she assaults men, kills or steals infants, scatters
sickness and death, antithetically she's demonic and heroic, a harlot
and mother, an irresistible blue-eyed blonde seductress and a "goggle-
eyed, hairy-legged vampire"—Lilith lives in allegories of terror and

desire, she's the primal female—fandom users enjoy arguing about who
she was and is, and recently an admirer posted: "World's first feminist
was demonized in lore? I'm not surprised. She just wanted to be treated
as an equal and was punished for it, so she took revenge. GO LILITH !!!"
And so Lilith goes, the first woman endlessly seducing imaginations.

## Monstrous Females

Mythology's packed with them, monstrous females,
heartless, soulless, murderous creatures in feminine
form, nightmarish fantasies of fear and desire—first,
there's Echidna, mother of monsters, a fierce
flesh-eating goddess, half-woman and half-snake,
the female half gorgeous, the snake half hideous,
she lived in a cave with Typhon, also half-snake,

who had 100 heads and breathed fire, and together
they spawned hundreds more monsters, Cerebus,
Chimera, Hydra, Sphinx, and Scylla among them—
a strange mix of terrors, Chimera had a lion's head
and body, a fire-breathing goat's head protruding
 from its back, and a serpent for a tail—Scylla had
12 feet and 6 heads on long snake-like necks, each

head had triple rows of shark-like teeth, ravenous,
she devoured sailors who strayed within her reach—
across a narrow strait, just an arrow shot away,
was Charybdis, another female monster, she
swallowed huge amounts of water and belched it all
out again, sinking ships and drowning men—then
there's the Gorgons, three most repulsive sisters,

each having tangles of venomous snakes for hair,
wings, claws, tusks, and scales, their looks could kill—
Medusa, The Queen, was once a beautiful maiden,
but was punished for having sex with Neptune and was
pregnant with the god's child when Perseus beheaded
her—unlike their mortal sister, Stheno and Euryale were
chthonic and eternal, Stheno, the eldest, The Mighty,

had brass hands and sharp fangs and killed more men
than both her sisters—known for her raucous bellowing,
Euryale, second oldest, the Far Springer, could crumble
stone into sand with her horrible howling—also a female
monster, the Sphinx feasted on Theban youths unable
to answer her riddles, she had a lion's body, eagle wings,
and a serpent's tail, but a woman's head and breasts—

Harpies, loathsome and disgusting creatures, were
half girl, half bird, human vultures with horrid faces
and sharp claws, constantly craving human flesh,
their breath was vile, their smell was repulsive,
and their excrement was putrid, yet some sources
note their hair was long and fair and their breasts
comely—similarly half bird, half girl creatures, Sirens

were alluring and beguiling, daughters of the sea,
they lived on rocky isles and lured sailors to their
deaths on treacherous rocks with their seductive
songs, the sailors helpless, desperate to get closer—
less abominable but more insatiable, Maenads,
the mad women, the raving ones, were followers
of Dionysus, dancing and drinking, they roamed

the mountains and forests during their orgiastic
frenzies, tearing animals and men to pieces—also
wandering the wilds, nymphs were female spirits,
minor goddesses, young and beautiful, irresistible
yet inaccessible, besotted with infatuation, men went
mad with desire—there's some sameness in these
horrors, savage females devouring impotent men.

# The Kelpie

A curious creature that lives in the whispers
of children, the warnings of parents, inhabiting
water and land, malevolent and murderous,
a shapeshifter, mostly a black horse inhabiting
the deep pools of rivers, streams, and lochs,
but sometimes a white horse or a tame pony,
and sometimes a beautiful young woman,

or a handsome young man, at times even
a wizened old man, all appearances to lure
the unwary to watery deaths, usually children
and lovestruck young adults, drowning them
in the depths, the dark waters, then devouring
them, livers and hearts dainty delicacies, but
 entrails are thrown back on the shore—stories

are centuries old and universal, those of Scottish
lore the best known, nearly every body of water
has them, even Loch Ness, its murky waters
ever a mystery, its second monster—a malevolent
water spirit, the horse has sticky skin, cold as death,
when touched humans cannot get loose, children
climb on for a ride and are carried off to drown,

those enchanted willingly take of the hand of alluring
strangers and are dragged to sodden deaths, never
to be seen again—Kelpie tales instruct children to be
cautious of dangerous waters, of seductive strangers,
of the evil hidden in smiles—Still, the Kelpie seduces,
existing in myth, children's books, souvenir shops,
and art, in Falkirk there's a 100-foot Kelpie statue.

## Succubi Still Exist

They existed for centuries, embraced in lore
and literature, in night terrors and sleep
disturbances, succubi, powerful female
demons assaulting sleeping men, stealing
their semen, dark hellish fantasies mingling
horror and desire, victims awake but paralyzed,
conscious but helpess, unable to move, who

wake drained, scared, distressed—priests
and rabbis unable to help, incantations,
potions, and amulets unable to subdue
demonic lust—variously described, some
as horrid fiends with claws, scales, and tails,
vulvas dripping vile fluids, some as beautiful
sirens charming and captivating helpless

men, some sources claim succubi need
sperm to survive, others assert they
transfer it to their infernal counterparts,
incubi, who use it to impregnate sleeping
women to produce cambions, demonic
half humans, tainting humanity with ungodly
seed, birth defects were once thought

to result from demon sex—today succubi
are more popular than ever, fashionable
and marketable, instead of the disgusting,
deformed sex-crazed female demons
of medieval texts, who had gargoyle faces,
noxious breath and stench, and claws
for hands and feet, succubi generally

are now depicted as beguiling, ravishing
enchantresses, glamorous and voluptuous,
whose wispy garments reveal more than
conceal, who embrace their strength,
their demonic natures, who enjoy their
powers to manipulate men, and who
inhabit legions of books and comic books,

cartoons, anime, games and MMORPGs,
films, plays, paintings, sculptures, songs
social media, and comicon cosplay events,
Wikipedia's list of succubi media is endless,
and Amazon offers equally endless varieties
of media, plus t-shirts, hoodies, horns, shoes,
costumes, sexy lingerie, temporary tattoos,

posters, figures and game miniatures,
both metal and resin, and jewelry—sixty
percent of all people suffer from sleep
paralysis, regaining consciousness but
unable to move, who wake exhausted
and anxious—tracking succubi's popularity
leaves one equally exhausted and anxious.

# A French Pope and His Demon Lover

More than four and a half centuries after he
died, a monk painted him with the Devil
in an illuminated manuscript, the Pope
is smiling, opening his arms, the horned,
cloven-footed, multi-faced Devil scowls
at the embrace, but numerous, slanderous
stories have been recounted of the two

consorting, most composed by two
Englishmen, a courtier and a monk, one
hundred years after he died—Gerbert of
Aurillac, who became Pope Sylvester II,
who supposedly learned the dark arts
while studying in Spain, who supposedly
stole an ungodly book of demonic sorcery

from a Saracen magician and hid under
a bridge, suspended between heaven
and earth, to escape, and with the secrets
of Hell he built a brass head, a mechanical
 Mephistopheles, to conjure forbidden
knowledge, infinite depths of the abyss,
but the most salacious stories concern

his love affair with Meridiana, a succubus,
who lay with him at night in infernal embrace,
who helped him ascend the throne of Rome,
but supposedly, before death, fearing eternal
perdition, he confessed his hellish affair
and died repentant, only to be resurrected
 in slander, the holiest office defiled by

the basest corruption—yet what's known, he
was one of the greatest scholars of his time,
regaining erudition in forgotten books, after
studying in Spain, he promoted Moorish
and classical learning, especially mathematics
and astronomy, he reintroduced the abacus
and the armillary sphere to Europe, both lost

for centuries, in Rheims he constructed an organ
that surpassed all previous instruments, as pope,
he opposed church corruption, especially simony
and concubinage—despite advancing humanity's
grasp, his remembrance is tainted with stains
and smears, and his scandalous love affair,
human and demon united, is immortalized online.

# Dame Alice Kyteler, Ireland's First Condemned Witch

An uncommon woman, appearing and disappearing in the early
fourteenth century, the first woman accused of acquiring magical
powers by having sex with a demon, the first woman tried for
witchcraft as a heretic, the first woman in Ireland condemned
for witchcraft, whose case caused a decade's long battle between

secular and sacred powers, who became the Bishop of Ossory's
personal crusade to advance Church sovereignty by damning her,
Alice Kyteler married four times, and each time acquiring her
husband's wealth and property, her stepchildren, outraged at
penurious inheritance, accused her of maleficium in the Bishop's

court, of using sorcery to seduce their fathers, beguiling them
of their estates, and emasculating them—ambitious to prove his
zeal and anxious to wield his inquisitional license, the tearing
and burning of flesh, and to launch his holy war, the Bishop
declared his Kilkenny diocese a hotbed of demons and witches

and charged Dame Alice with heresy, witchery, and depravity—
excommunicating and condemning her on seven charges, 1) she
denied Christ and the Church, 2) she sacrificed chickens, scattering
blood and bone at crossroads, a horrid offering to Robert, her
demon lover, 3) she stole the church keys and at night held hellish

sabbaths, casting spells and offering vile maledictions to corrupt
Christians and subvert the Church, 4) she brewed a devilish mix
of chicken intestines, worms, hair from the buttocks of boys who
died before baptism, and fingernail clippings trimmed from the dead,
and 5) she had intercourse with Robert, who appeared as a cat,

a shaggy black dog, and a black man, fiendish carnal knowledge
to obtain wealth and power, 6) to fly at night she rubbed infernal
ointment on a stick, and 7) she besot her husbands with sordid
lust and used devilish sorcery to murder them and snatched
their substance to impoverish her stepchildren—Alice fled, first

to Dublin, then perhaps London, disappearing from public records,
yet the Bishop vented his inflamed passion on Petronella, her
maidservant, torturing her to confess she witnessed execrable

abominations, malefic sacrifices summoning Robert, the demon lover, from the depths of hell, that horrid witch's brew, that once

she watched her lady have sex with Robert and afterwards her lady used the soiled sheets to wipe away the ungodly slime, in return for her confessions, the Bishop had Petronella publicly whipped seven times and, on November 3, 1324, he had her burned at the stake, a kindness to prepare her for hell's eternal

flames—for decades more the Bishop carried on his crusade— though having disappeared from history Alice has reappeared, Yeats mentions her in a poem, "the love-lorn Lady Kyteler," and Eco alludes to her in *The Name of the Rose*, she's sighted in several novels and stories, and dozens of law books reference her trial,

she's featured in several dozen YouTube videos as Ireland's first witch, and Google provides 1,750,000 search results, and today in Kilkenny there's the Kyteler's Inn, where visitors can drink "Alice's Spirit," a local whiskey, eat Irish stew, listen to live music, then have their photo taken next to a statue of Dame Alice holding a broom.

# Isobel Gowdie's Four Confessions: Spokin and Willinglie Confest in 1662

Probably, she was strangled then burned,
dispatched to her master, her lover, the Devil,
but records offer little, her death, her life, lost,
furtive mists glimpsed then gone, the wife
of a farm laborer, tenants of tenants kept
by the Laird of the Park, living near a small
village near another small village, day after
day constant labor, the struggle to get on,

Isobel Gowdie was unable to read or write, yet
a gifted storyteller, during the Great Scottish
Witch Hunt, she confessed four times over six
weeks, confessions exceptionally rich in inequity,
perhaps already accused she confessed to save
herself, or perhaps to torment the local vicar,
a zealot who feared women and witchcraft, who
disdained her worth, no one knows, probably

she was tortured, perhaps—with ministers
and magistrates leering—stripped and stabbed
repeatedly by a witch pricker searching
for the Devil's mark, her wild words taken
from her mouth, a minister transcribed, her
interrogators, astonished, aghast, damned her
with questions, yet she willingly confessed,

confessing far more than they hoped for, mixing
fairies and demons, she narrated lurid tales
of blasphemy, depravity, and necromancy, and sex
with Satan, a devilish orgy at night in a church,
his monstrous genitalia described, his coupling
rough, cold, and pleasureless, renouncing her
baptism, she kneeled to offer the anal kiss, she

joined a coven, dined with the Faerie Queen, caroused
with devils, murdered with elf arrows, and conjured
an infernal horse from corn silk—her confessions are
described as some "of the most remarkable in the history

of witchcraft" and as "the most comprehensive insights into European witchcraft folklore," though storytelling her only power, she is celebrated as The Witch Queen of Scotland.

# Never A Normal Life: Mother Shipton, A Sybil in North Yorkshire

Never a normal life, never a chance to live like others,
Mother Shipton, born in a cave, her mother a fifteen-year-
old orphan, her father unknown, and physically different,
hunchback, long crooked nose, crooked legs, goggle—
eyed, mother and infant scorned by the townspeople,
the stories started at birth, born during a fierce
thunderstorm, the Devil her father, her laugh a witch's

cackle, shunned and demonized, a child called hag
face, the Devil's bastard, spawn of Satan—mother
and daughter lived in the cave until an abbot intervened,
mother sent to a nunnery, daughter placed in a family,
but never accepted, always an outcast, believed to be
a witch, yet at 24 she married a local carpenter, but
still the whispers—she bewitched him—two years later

he died, and the villagers, her neighbors, accused
her of killing him—taunted and teased she took
to the woods, back to her cave, her sanctuary, away
from rumors and stares, the unkind words, and there
she thrived, gathering plants for herbal remedies,
people came to her seeking her potions, her spells,
a few then many, a most gracious witch, her fame

increased, and she began to divine the future,
a Sybil in a grotto, offering visions with tinctures,
even Henry VIII heard of her, the Witch of York,
dying in 1561 she lived in folktales, eighty years
later her first book of prophecies appeared,
followed by many more, stories becoming life,
her cave becoming England's first tourist attraction.

# Mary Lee, Bound for a New Life

Not a lot is known about her, Mary Lee, only
that in 1654 she boarded the Charity bound
for a new life in Maryland, but her life ended
three weeks or so before the ship arrived,
manhandled by sailors, in frenzy and fear, her
breath choked out of her by a rope, hanged
for being a witch, her body and belongings

tossed overboard to calm the stormy seas,
condemned by contrary winds and violent
squalls, rumor and rage, terror and panic,
a difficult voyage in perilous waters, what
new life in a new land she conjured is not
known, or what provoked the suspicions,
the accusations, but with successive storms

the sailors grew agitated, and mutterings
increased, fearing his crew, Captain Bosworth
said he'd put her ashore in Bermuda, but
winds and storms pushed the Charity off
course, "and the Ship grew daily more leaky
almost to desperation," a Jesuit on board,
Father Francis, later declared the sailors

believed the foul weather was caused
by "the malevolence of witches," and they
accused her because of her "deportment
and discourse"—they "importuned the Said
Master that a trial might be had of her," but
the Bosworth refused, and two sailors, whose
names are unknown, taking the matter into

their hands, stripped and searched Mary Lee,
and found what they were looking for, "Some
Signall or Marke of a witch," the witch's teat,
or skin tag, or blemish, or whatever, they
called for "others to See it" and bound her
"betwixt decks" overnight, interrogating her
until "She confessed as by her Confession

appeareth," such sad words later collected
by the Council of Maryland, the sailors implored
Bosworth "to put her to Death"—Thou shalt
not suffer a witch to live—yet he declined,
but "being more Vehemently pressed to it,
he tould them they might do what they would,"
and went below to his cabin, the sailors "laying

all their hands" on her, dragged her before
the yardarm, and soon after "these words (She
is dead) ran out," when told "they have hanged her,"
Bosworth "Speaking with trouble in a high Voyce
replyed he knew not of it," and "Commanded
they Should doe Nothing without his Order."

# III. There Are Three Deaths

## What the Aztecs Believed

I
There are three deaths, the first
your last breath, the second your
burial, and the third when no
one remembers your name.

II
The death whistle shrieks, a soul
ripped from life, a howling wind,
maybe used to intimidate those
attacked, maybe used at human
sacrifice, a 20-year-old victim's
finger bones clutched a death whistle.

III
They believed in afterlife, those who
died violent deaths, in battle or sacrifice,
went to Tlalocan, glowing with eternal
springs, the fourth of thirteen heavens,
wrapped in burial cloth decorated
with hummingbirds and butterflies, they
were honored by the sun god, whose
rays guided them their place in paradise.

IV
Those who died unremarkable deaths,
 illness or old age, went to Mictlan,
a dark underworld ruled by a skeletal
death god, these dead were wrapped
in cloth and cremated with a dog,
a guide and companion in the underworld,
their grueling journey took four years
to reach the deepest layer of the abyss.

V
The dead were assigned jobs to serve
the gods, the work assigned had nothing
to do how well they lived, but how well they
died, death the driving force of life, a grim,
harsh life—life merely momentarily loaned.

VI
Women who died in childbirth were held
in high status, and honored as warriors, they
traveled west to the female half of heaven,
where they helped ease the sun down
into darkness, their bodies divine, warriors—
seeking courage in battle—took their fingers
and hair to adorn their shields, unhappy at
not being a mother, some haunted the living,
a mere glimpse of a ghost caused seizures.

VII
Death extended life, humans were sacrificed
to maintain balance in the cosmos, to ensure
the sun would rise and rain would fall,
children were sacrificed to repay the gods
for rain that nourished their crops, sacrifice
was widespread, but reports exaggerated,
at the Grand Pyramid in 1487 supposedly
10,000 to 80,000 were sacrificed in four days,
their hearts torn out with obsidian knives,
their bodies thrown down the bloody steps.

VIII
Starting in 1545, 15 million Aztecs died
within 5 years, all unremarkable deaths,
over three quarters of the population,
wiped out by cocoliztli, the Aztec word
for pestilence, the most devastating
of three plagues, gifts of the conquerers,
one of the deadliest in human history,
second only to the Black Death, high fevers,
headaches, bleeding from the eyes, mouth,
and ears, death in 3 to 4 days, an enteric
fever, the living scarcely able to bury the dead.

# Dancing with the Dead

Always, there's been seekers,
believers of secret knowledge,
followers of the Blazing Star,
the All-Seeing Eye, the Great
Architect of the Universe,
the Book of Enoch, the books
of Moses, pursuers of mystical

learning and gnostic illumination,
aching to grasp God's mysteries,
believing inviolable truths are
concealed from humanity unfit
for the shock of perception,
pursuing cryptic conjunctions
of numbers and letters, stars

and planets, roses and crosses,
hidden codes, ciphers, and glyphs
of eternal verities, transcendent
awakenings and occult enigmas
of golden dawns and silver light,
theosophical societies longing
for divine union, for concealed

veils to be lifted and invisible
pathways uncovered, they've
tried magnets, magic lanterns,
and redemption machines, as well
as elixirs, emetics, roots, runes,
crystals, candles, tonics, potions,
and totems, also fasting, flogging,

scarring, and burning, dancing,
whirling, chanting, and drumming,
countless prayers have been uttered,
and countless deities and demons
implored, from alpha to omega there's
been sensual indulgence and ascetic

denial, chastity and promiscuity,
abstinence and drunkenness, those
longing to be struck with knowing
have used poisons and hallucinogens,
curses and cures, dolls, pentacles,
candles, rituals, and spells, they've

observed the moon wax and wane,
the flight of birds, the flow of tides,
they've read cards, smoke, dice,
entrails, livers, eggs, arrows, spilled
wine, and tea leaves to seek celestial
connections, the bearers of light,
they've built altars and made offerings

to embrace the promise of love,
gnosticism, hermeticism, kabbalism,
and esoterism, the belief in ancient
wisdom, in meaning beyond reason,
in learning what none can learn,
in having what none can have—so
many paths but only one destination.

# The Devil's Pitchfork

Walmart offers them online as costume accessories,
long or short, with or without spikes or sequins,
countless variations of red and black, the devil's
pitchfork, all reasonably priced, Amazon peddles
hundreds in various shapes and sizes, some come
with sexy red devil costumes, and some "with scary
Pronged Forks with fake blood and realistic faux

Wood," even as jewelry, small barbels of surgical
steel suitable for body piercings—But when did
devils and demons pick up pitchforks to torment
lost souls? Those early church patriarchs never
described devils wielding pitchforks, herding
the damned and doomed into eternal hellfire—
the earliest representation comes a thousand years

later, a 10th-century carving in an Irish monastery
depicting a devil with pitchfork in hand, forcing
mortals away from Jesus, accompanied by a blast
of a demon's trumpet, a hellish parade destined
for fiery pits of infinite agony and endless remorse,
soon images of devils prodding, jabbing, stabbing
lost souls became conventional in illuminated

manuscripts, monks and their codices, painstaking
and delicate handwork of the accursed racked with
unbearable misery, a demonic inversion of John
the Baptist: "His winnowing fork in his hand . . .
gathering his wheat into the barn and burning up
the chaff with unquenchable fire"—pitchforks were
common enough, both tools and weapons, angry

peasant mobs carried torches and pitchforks while
pursuing demons, werewolves, vampires, and witches
at night, or when going off to war for distant lords,
a most serviceable instrument for separating grain
and souls— being associated with devils, the English
disdained forks for several centuries, preferring to use
knives, spoons, and hands at meals, considering them

an Italian fashion, a foppish affectation, Queen Elizabeth
had forks but preferred eating with her fingers, declaring
"spearing an uncouth action"—Emperor Otto's wife had
first brought forks to Europe in the 10th century, and by
the 14th century forks had become fashionable among
the merchant classes—when Catherine de'Medici arrived
in France to marry Henry II, the future King, she brought

forks along with her Florentine chefs, a long list of foods
and recipes, and a retinue of maids to help manage her
lavish wardrobe—and slowly, like grass lawns and ornate
gardens, forks became popular among the elite, then later
among commoners, until most everyone had forks, except
the English, who continued to distrust them as devilish,
and who proudly persisted with their fingers until, finally,

King Charles I proclaimed, "It is decent to use a fork," but
many remained suspicious of the tiny pitchforks, especially
colonists across the Atlantic-- when he arrived in 1630, John
Winthrop, the most Puritan of the Puritans and the first
Governor of the Bay Colony, shocked his pious brethren when
he was seen with a fork, but it was not until after the Revolution
that Americans routinely began picked up the Devil's tool.

# Hermes Trismegistus: The Most Famous Man Alive Who Never Lived

He lived for centuries but was never alive,
and for a time, for seekers of ancient wisdom,
he was the most famous man alive, Hermes
Trismegistus, Hermes the Thrice-Greatest,
he was a man, a god, or two gods syncretized
into one all-powerful, all-knowing deity—
scholars dispute his numerous identities,

his various legends, his myriad sources, all affixed
to one cryptic name—he lived before and after
the Flood, he invented hieroglyphics to preserve
his wisdom, he translated his divine wisdom
into Greek to entice humanity's transcendence,
he built the pyramids, he was Adam's grandson,
he was a contemporary of Moses, and of Jesus,

he was Enoch who pleaded with God to save
the fallen angels for their dalliance with mortal
women, he was the Islamic prophet Idris, he was
Cadmus, founder of Thebes, he created I Ching,
he founded the German people, he created
civilization, giving humanity "medicine, chemistry
writing, laws, art, astrology, music, magic, rhetoric,

philosophy, geography, mathematics, and much
more," variously, he was thought to have written
42 books, 20,000 books, or even 36,000 books,
in one of these books, the legendary *Book
of Thoth*, he revealed the secrets of immortality—
from the Middle Ages to the Renaissance he
was a real person, the Egyptian, who started

the long chain of hermetic writings containing
the single, true revelation, the secrets of God—
the luminous Word of creation, the divine
spark, the path to ascension, the hidden
knowledge that leads to salvation, celestial
utterance that had been lost, pieces of God
concealed from humanity's corruption—

known only to a few prophets, cryptic knowledge
coded in words, numbers, symbols, stars,
and ceremonial magic—Hermes Trismegistus,
God's scrivener, celestial influencer, quickly fell
from grace, his immense influence reduced
to ridicule when Humanist scholars discovered
his mysterious writings were not God's first

words, when science displaced magic,
yet the quest continues, seekers in secret
yet believe there is knowing without knowledge,
and not knowing what they want to know,
they yet pursue the Philosopher's Stone,
hermetically sealed—gnostic enlightenment
beyond human noise—to recreate the Creator.

# John Gee, The Queen Called Him "My Philosopher"

Once a mighty man, once advisor to Queen Elizabeth,
John Dee died in poverty, and his gravesite's unknown,
mathematician and magician, astronomer and astrologer,
occultist, alchemist, and imperialist, he believed numbers
were magical, keys to divine communion, the mystical
union of all creation, a seeker of hidden knowledge,
natural and supernatural, enlightenment in darkness,

science in a sorcerer's scryer, he gazed into crystals
to communicate with angels and recorded their words
in indecipherable language, a believer in these spiritual
conferences, he obeyed when the archangel of wisdom,
Uriel, ordered him to share his wife with a charlatan—
a seeker of secret texts, he amassed England's largest
private library and then, to keep from starving, sold

it book by book, he wrote *Monas Hieroglyphica*,
a Heremtic text to heal all schisms, esteemed by
contemporaries yet unreadable today—he coined
the term "British Empire," and wrote the *Perfect Arte
of Navigation* to help England spread its domain—
for casting horoscopes for Princess Elizabeth
and Queen Mary, he was arrested for "calculating,"

a treasonable crime, exonerated in court but never
from slander, he pursued a perpetual motion machine,
magic gems, spirit mirrors, a celestial alphabet,
the Seal of God, the mysteries of Heaven—a Christian,
thaumaturgist and necromancist, a weaver of signs,
symbols, and numbers to summon spirits, an ethereal
web, he was a real-life Prospero and melted into thin air.

# Matthew Hopkins, Witch Finder General

Both book and death arrived together in 1647,
he only 27, but his life overrun with egregious
righteousness shrouding cruelty and cupidity,
his book his defense against a court's charges,
*The Discovery of Witches* sold well, multiple
editions over time, and still is available at eBay,
Walmart, and Amazon, both paper and hardbound,

often with his original frontispiece, an engraving
depicting his calling, his image beneath his assumed
title, Witch Finder General, a rakish young gentleman
well-dressed in boots, cape, collar, puritan hat, holding
a long staff, and before him two confessed witches
naming their hellish imps, Vinegar Tom, Pyewackett,
Grizzell Greedigut, Illemauzer, Pecke, and Jamara,

bizarre names and grotesque creatures, the strange
scene justifying his trade—in the midst of civil war
and chaos, the rule of law broken, claiming the land
awash with witches, towns crowded with devils,
suspicions and accusations rampant, he and his retinue
roamed East Anglia selling their services, in two short
years they sent over 100 alleged witches to the gallows,

more hanged for witchcraft than in the previous 100
years, more than all other witch finders, defenseless
victims, mostly poor, uneducated women—their work
paid well, towns paying around $4000 plus expenses,
huge sums back then, taxes were levied to cover the fees,
*The Discovery* defended their methods, citing King James,
not the Bible, the accused stripped, shaved, and searched

for the Devil's Mark, the unnatural teat where familiars
sucked—since witches do not bleed, the accused were
cut with blunt knives, tormented, threatened, deprived
of sleep, confessions were forced, the witch finder general
favored the notorious swimming test, arms and legs
bound to a chair, the accused tossed into water, those
who drowned were innocent and received into heaven,

Hopkins was finally called to court in Norfolk to explain his witch-finding, accused of tormenting those he accused with "an abominable, inhumane and unmercifull tryall of those poore creatures, by tying them, and heaving them into the water, a tryall not allowable by Law or conscience," he died soon after, and his death led to a "pleasing legend" that he had been subjected to his own swimming test.

# Aleister Crowley, The Wickedest Man in the World

His mother called him The Beast, not affectionately, newspapers reviled him as "wickedest man in the world," "the King of Depravity," "one of the most blasphemous and cold-blooded villains of modern times," "a man we'd like to hang," and "scum"—stories of his deviance and decadence spread around the world, he was evil incarnate, a degenerate, a hedonist, a drug addict, a sex

fiend, and a satanist, Yeats declared him to be "indescribably mad," Aleister Crowley, born into wealth and luxury, died in poverty and obscurity, yet in 2002 a BBC survey listed him 73rd in a list of the 100 Greatest Britons, and he's cited as a pervasive influence on seekers of mystical knowledge, spiritual enlightenment, and magical practice, on occultism and neopaganism, his lasting impact has been compared

to Freud and Jung, and in popular culture he's a figure of fascination, appearing on the Sgt. Pepper's album cover and in the lyrics of Led Zeppelin, David Bowie, and Ozzy Osborne—rock'n'roll always the devil's music—he delighted in disruption and opposition, the destruction of Victorian morality and hypocrisy, the voiding of Christianity, a "slave religion," his family's fundamentalism a favorite target,

perverse and contrary, devoted to the unfettered pursuit of self-indulgence, of supreme self-fulfillment, influenced by social Darwinism, Nietzsche, and Swedenborg, he created his own religion—Thelema (Greek for will), and declared himself a prophet preordained to liberate humanity from its spiritual subjugation, his creed's central doctrine— Do What Thou Wilt—urged all to undertake their Great

Work, the discovery of their True Will, drugs, sex, blood sacrifice, and sadomasochism pathways to divine transcendence—loathing his birth name, Edward Alexander, he adopted Aleister at 20 because it was "the most favourable name for becoming famous," an insistent lifelong desire— during his Cairo honeymoon, Horus, the falcon-headed god, sent him an emissary, Aiwass, who dictated *The Book*

*of the Law*, Thelema's holy book, to usher in a new age,
the Aeon of Horus, Aiwass sometimes identified as Satan—
peripatetic and unsettled, yet unwavering in his personal
pursuits, he never had many followers, only a few followed
him to the Abbey of Thelema, a farmhouse in Sicily, where
Crowley, his wife, his mistress, their children, and disciples
practiced sex magic, consumed narcotics and stimulants,

sacrificed small animals, and summoned spirits, the Abbey
his "idea of heaven," but after a young Oxford student died,
Crowley was denounced in British newspapers—the death
blamed on a magical ritual involving the guzzling of cat's
blood—Mussolini, detesting degenerates, had him deported—
despite heroin addiction and poor health, he filled his life
with debauchery and adultery (his long train of lovers

both male and female), scandals, mystical retreats, court
cases (being sued and suing), promoting Thelema,
and publishing—the number of his children and printed
works unclear—he was a poet, novelist, metaphysicist,
occultist, and writer of pornographic potboilers (*The Diary
of a Drug Fiend*), his death in 1947 at 72 mostly a good
riddance, yet in the 60s, as supernatural and metaphysical

interests exploded, he was brought back to life, appearing
in numerous novels, plays, songs, and now video games,
his displays of disruption and opposition appealing to
those embracing the wildness of punk, anarchy, and chaos,
to those seeking magical power and pagan gods, Crowley
now has more followers than in life, yet in 2010 his Abbey
was listed for sale at 1.5 million Euro—but went unsold.

# IV. Indecent Exhibitions

# Empress Theodora, The Most Powerful Woman in Byzantium

*Britannica* speculates she was "probably the most
powerful woman in Byzantium history," she was
her husband's chief advisor, the Emperor Justinian,
and her influence was immense, some speculate
that from 527 until her death (possibly breast cancer)
in 548, she, and not he, ruled the Eastern Empire,
her name appears in nearly every piece of legislation

passed while she was Empress, she met with foreign
envoys and corresponded with foreign heads of state,
she required government officials to prostrate
before her and kiss both feet, a sign of magisterial
deference, for her good works she was canonized
a saint in the Eastern Orthodox Church, and her day
is still celebrated, yet she was not of royal blood,

and her life was narrated in distorted slurs and slander,
scurrilous stories caricatured in Procopius's *Secret
History*, a specious text written by a disillusioned
historian, her early years spent in the Hippodrome,
that wild circus of amusements, where her father was
a bear trainer for the Greens and her stepfather
a bear trainer for the Blues, irascible factions—barely

a teenager she worked in a Constantinople brothel
and performed as an actress in the Hippodrome, her
pornographic portrayals of Leda and the Swan were
particularly popular, she danced naked on stage except
for a loose ribbon, and reclining on a couch, she had
 geese peck barley grains from her genitals, while performing
these "indecent exhibitions" she continued barter carnal

services offstage, leading Gibbon centuries later to cite her
as another example of Roman depravity leading to the fall:
"when she passed through the streets her presence was
avoided by all who wished to escape either the scandal
or the temptation," while still a teen she traveled to North
Africa as a Syrian official's concubine but was mistreated
and fled, in Alexandria she converted to Miaphysitism,

embracing Christ as fully flesh and fully divine in one physis,
destitute, she might have worked as a wool spinner, in Antioch
she might have met a dancer for the Blues, who might have
been Justinian's spy, returning to Constantinople she met
Justinian, who—enamored by her beauty and intelligence—
proposed, but a law forbade men of high rank marrying
disreputable actresses, and a new law was decreed to allow

the marriage to take place in 525—when Justinian became
Emperor two years later, Thoedora was crowned *augusta*,
Procopius asserts that they ruled jointly, quoting Justinian
as declaring Theodora was "a partner in my deliberations,"
a most singular and strange statement for an emperor
at a time when women had little status or power, together
they built and rebuilt Constantinople, building aqueducts,

bridges, public structures, and at least 25 churches, visible
public works that the common people loved, but nobles,
"strangled with taxes," did not, yet Empress and Emperor
attempted to heal deep divides among classes and factions,
they advanced social reforms, fought corruption, improved
the legal system, and made the streets safer, Byzantine's
golden age, Theodora championed the causes of girls

sold into prostitution, buying them from their servitude
and establishing a convent for their rehabilitation, leading
one commentor to declare: she "freed the girls from the yoke
of their wretched slavery," aligned with the senatorial ranks
that opposed high taxes, Procopius stated the Empress
merely had 500 prostitutes "rounded up" and dumped
in a convent, but the women resented their "unwelcome

transformation" and escaped by climbing over the cloister's
walls—unlike Gibbon, today most historians view the *Secret
History* as an unreliable source and concur Theodora was
active in promoting the rights of women in divorce, property
ownership, and child guardianship, prohibiting the traffic
of young girls, making rape a capital offence and adultery
laws more just, today *Britannica* and many other sources

commend Theodora as "one of the first rulers to recognize
the rights of women," but Procopius—constantly carping—
claimed that in promoting women she accomplished
the opposite, causing them "to become morally depraved,"

yet the *Secret History* says as much about the author as Emperor and Empress, a court historian horrified by the misappropriation of roles, by women ruling.

# The Hippodrome of Constantinople

For centuries the city's social center, to see and be
seen, to sell and seduce, boundless pleasures
and entertainments were nonstop, the Hippodrome
was a circus, zoo, sporting arena, amusement
park, amphitheater, marketplace, political
forum, and battleground, commoners mingled
with patricians, emperors entertained dignitaries

while prostitutes, actresses, and bears performed,
civil ceremonies, religious rituals, and pornographic
performances all meshed together, no separation
of church and state here, where chariot races ruled
the empire, Constantine the Great lavishly rebuilt
it in the 4th century, filling the racetrack's center
with bronze statues and marble obelisks, the stands

could hold 100,000 spectators, and huge sums were
bet and bitter rivalries evolved between the race
teams, the Blues and the Greens, each sponsored
by different factions fomenting constant intrigues,
eight chariots pulled by four horses raced around
the U-shaped track, the outcomes deciding destinies—
beatings, murders, and riots were not uncommon,

during the Nika Riot around 30,000 were killed
and dozens of buildings destroyed, civil wars were
fought in the Hippodrome, but Justinian and Theodora
lavishly rebuilt what was destroyed, yet the city never
recovered after being sacked in 1204 during the Fourth
Crusade, when Mehmed the Conqueror captured the city,
and its races, riots, and profuse pleasures were forbidden.

# Something More Than I Was: Margot of Valois, Queen of France

*"All the harm that ever came to me in life came through marriage. Do not let anyone say that marriages are made in heaven: the gods would not commit so great an injustice."*

—Margaret of Valois,
*Memoires et Lettres de Margerite de Valois*

Daughter of a king, sister of three kings, wife of a king,
and twice a queen, Margaret of Valois was destined
for eminence, nurtured in power and privilege, unusual
even for a royal female, she was well-educated, highly
cultivated, spoke five languages, and accomplished
not only in etiquette, dance, and horsemanship, but
 also in philosophy, prose, and poetry, a woman

of letters who, in repudiating misogyny, published
The *Learned and Subtle Discourse* arguing women were
superior to men, and she wrote one of the first ever
female-authored memoirs, she was a benefactor
of the poor and a patron of the arts, she surrounded
herself with scholars, writers, artists, and musicians, one
source states "her banquets and salons frequently hosted

the great minds of the time, and her household became
central to cultural, intellectual, and philosophical life,"
during France's Wars of Religion and murderous factions,
she acted as a mediator for peace, yet history has been
unkind to her memory, a pawn of politics and propaganda,
she was vilified by court rivals as being a nymphomaniac,
as being incestuous, of abandoned lewd and licentious

behavior whose flagrant affairs caused such scandal
that her own brother, King Henry III, banished her
from the royal court, an unprecedented scandal for
royals, a black legend evolved around her, or rather
her distortions, and legend eclipsed life, she became
a target for scurrilous pamphleteers, and wild tales
were told of her debaucheries to discredit all women

in political roles and later to denounce the depravity
of the *Ancien Régime,* Shakespeare's *Love's Labour's
Lost* loosely depicts her court, where king, queen,
and courtiers all compete in amorous adventures,
and Dumas's *La Reine Margot* sustains the black
legend to titillate readers, yet a strong woman who
never accepted her inferiority, and who took

an active role in the French affairs of state, she
prevailed despite court intrigues, broken alliances,
and treacherous conspiracies, despite her family
constantly at war with itself, despite being abused
by mother and brother, despite her body being
royal property, her virginity a commodity, despite
her marriage—intended to secure peace—igniting

the St. Bartholomew's Day Massacre, France's
bloodiest mass slaughter, despite being persecuted
by brother and husband, Kings Henry III and Henry IV,
despite the assassinations of both Henrys, despite
an arrest for a coup d'etat and being forced to watch
the execution of her lover (the black legend declares
she kept the pickled head), despite being imprisoned

in exile, despite being unable to bear a royal heir and being
ridiculed for infertility, despite the numerous betrayals
in a game of thrones when gentility masked treachery,
despite ribald rumors obscuring intellectual discourse,
despite fandom sites where myths persist, where Margot
shrouds Margaret, and despite her casket being lost
or stolen—historians are recovering her misplaced life.

# The Saint Bartholomew's Day Massacre:
# "The Worst of the Century's Religious Massacres"

Accounts vary widely, the killers and the killed,
some go as high as 70,000 slaughtered, most range
between 5,000 and 30,000, neighbors butchering
neighbors, Christians killing Christians in the name
of Christ, the killings started in Paris, the most violently
anti-Huguenot city, where Huguenot leaders had gathered
for a wedding, the nuptials to secure a shaky peace,

a Catholic princess marrying a Protestant prince, yet
three days of merciless slaughter erupted, thousands
of corpses in the streets were carted off and dumped
in the Seine, the bloodshed soon spread across French
provinces, and for over 3 months the killings continued
in 12 other cities, accounts vary widely on the causes,
the instigators, and perpetrators, most believe Catherine

de' Medici, the Queen Mother, incited the atrocities,
she and her Italian advisers—4 days after the wedding
Admiral Coligny, the Huguenot leader, was shot in a street,
the assassin shooting from an upstairs window, the house
owned by Catholic adversaries, the city erupted into crisis,
and though the King and his courtiers visited the wounded
Protestant leader, promising swift justice, later that night

he met with the Queen Mother and together they
compiled a death list of Huguenot nobles, the King
then commanded his Swiss mercenaries to carry out his
orders, accounts vary, but on the eve of the Apostle's feast,
when bells rang for matins, the remorseless mercenaries
herded the nobles, their families, and their retinues
 into the streets outside the Louvre, murdering everyone,

soon Coligny was dragged from his bed and killed, his
body thrown out a window, his severed head paraded
through the city to inflame the mobs, who piously
believed their butchery was executing the will of God
and King—Catholics raced through the streets hunting
Protestants, the city gates were shut and streets were
barricaded to prevent escape, the bloodletting spiraled

out of control, women and children were not spared,
three days later—while the massacre continued—the King
appeared before the *Parlement de Paris*, justifying barbarous
mass murder as a timely, necessary expedient to preserve
peace and unity by preventing a Protestant plot against
France and the royal family, the most monstrous, heartless
political spinning masking savagery as salvation—with death

cries echoing in the streets a jubilee procession was held,
and all across France Catholic zealots celebrated the King's
kindness in preserving Christendom, when hearing the news
the King of Spain laughed with glee, in Rome the Pope sent
Charles IX a Golden Rose as a sign of his favor and requested
a *Te Deum*, where hymns of thanksgiving were sung,
and ordered a commemorative medal struck displaying

an avenging angel holding both cross and sword standing
exultantly before the corpses of murdered Protestants,
its celebratory inscription: "*Ugonottorum strages 1572*"
("Slaughter of the Huguenots 1572"), fervent Catholics
conceived the genocide as divine retribution for dangerous
heresy, as deliverance from imminent Protestant peril—
a war of words exploded in pulpits and in print, streams

of militant sermons and virulent polemics, one spurious
account, supposedly written by the King's brother, quoted
Charles IX: "Well, then, so be it! Kill them! But kill them
all! Don't leave a single one alive to reproach me," Catholic
apologists praised the murderous frenzy while outraged
Protestants painted Catholicism as a cruel, bloodthirsty
religion, one apologist absolved the blood-stained mobs:

"one must excuse the people's fury moved by laudable
zeal which is difficult to restrain once it has been stirred
up," and another defender rationalized the irrational
bloodbath as "a well-merited punishment for years
of civil disobedience and secret sedition"—sectarian
schisms sparked extreme estrangement and violence,
promoted extreme discord and disunion, paroxysms

of blind rage shattered the bonds of tolerance, union,
charity, and compassion, and once more religious wars
were reignited in France, and once more inhumanity
decimated humanity—exactly 425 years later, in 1997,

when celebrating World Youth Day in Paris, Pope John Paul II acknowledged the genocide: "we cannot forget the sad massacre . . . Christians did things the Gospel condemns."

## Madame de Pompadour: The Most Powerful Woman in France

She's an "iconic character in both French and world history," and during her brief life (1721-1764) she was "the most powerful woman in France and one of the most powerful in Europe," yet a *Smithsonian Magazine* article (2017) states "she's been historically overlooked," and her Wikipedia entry mentions several "historical misconceptions" that have maligned her memory, Jeanne-Antionette Poisson, known as Madame

de Pompadour, King Louis XV's most beloved mistress—for 20 years she lived at Versailles, first as "thirteenth lady-in-waiting," ultimately rising to become "lady-in-waiting," the most noble rank for a woman at court, she was the King's closest confidante, advisor, ally, and friend—as his de facto prime minister, she granted promotions and privileges, and she counseled on all matters of state,

domestic and foreign, even after she stopped having sex with the King (the result of three miscarriages, ill health, an unfortunate case of leucorrhea, and low libido—which a diet of truffles, celery, and vanilla failed to cure), she remained his constant companion, his indispensable collaborator—from a young age she had been cultivated to become the King's mistress, when she was 9, her

mother took her to Madame de Lebon, a fortuneteller, who predicted that she would one day reign over the heart of a king, and from then on her mother called her Reinette (Little Queen), a beautiful, intelligent young woman, she married at 19 and frequented the best Parisian salons, Louis XV surely heard of her appearances, but she plotted to catch his eye, while the King and his entourage were

hunting near her husband's estate, she twice crossed his path, first in a pink carriage wearing a blue dress, and next in a blue carriage wearing a pink dress, when they met at a masked ball (the King and 7 courtiers dressed as a yew tree, and she as Diana the Huntress), the King unmasked himself before her—he installed her at Versailles, gave her an estate, a title, and coat of arms, and she became *Marquise*

*de Pompadour*, the undisputed royal mistress—reticent
and shy, the King needed her, trusted her, to communicate
his will, by most accounts Louis XV's reign was disastrous
for France and led to *la Terreur* (the Reign of Terror)—after
the Seven Year's War (1756-1763), the government was
bankrupt, its American colonies lost, and its international
power and prestige in decline, and Madame de Pompadour

was blamed for the losses and was relentlessly attacked
by her many enemies, a commoner consorting with a King,
a woman meddling in politics, ruinous feminine influence,
supposedly—as her adversaries gleefully reported—after
the devastating losses at the Battle of Rossbach (1757),
she consoled the King with dismissive indifference: *"au reste,
après nous, le Déluge"* (besides, after us, the deluge

—nothing matters after we die), yet so much mattered,
deeply committed to France and French culture, she was
a vigorous patron of the arts, promoting countless painters,
sculptors, engravers, printers, jewelers, composers, writers,
actors and philosophers, under her direction Paris became
Europe's capital of taste, embracing the Enlightenment,
she befriended Voltaire and defended Diderot, she helped

spread the Rococo style across Europe—its exuberant
ornamentation intended to startle at first sight—today
pompadour refers to an unfashionable, poofy hairstyle,
and on Amazon there's pompadour combs, brushes,
pomades, powders, wigs, gowns, beard oil, and "Kiss So
Wispy Pompadour Eyelashes," there's even a fishing lure,
the "Jackall Pompadour"—she's everywhere and nowhere.

# Henry VIII Foully Imbued

By the time he was forty, Henry VIII weighed
four hundred pounds and was syphilitic, he suffered
putrefying leg sores and was carried around
in a sedan chair, towards the end, he ordered
a string of masses to save his soul, then declared
himself sinless—he wrote a mass, an essay
condemning divorce, supposedly the song

"Greensleeves" for Anne Boleyn, who he
later claimed bewitched him, and a riddle:
"What is it, that being born without life, head,
lip, or eye, yet doth go roaring throughout
the world till it die?" Yet he roared through
life, executing 72,000 people, including two
wives, legalized the killing of gypsies, devised

a new torture, pressing, and a new execution,
boiling—dying at 56, his last words, "monks,
monks, monks," those he dispossessed, two
weeks later he decanted when his lead coffin
burst, "All the pavement of the church," one
witness exclaimed, "was covered with fat and
the corrupt and putrefied blood foully imbued."

# Frederick the Great Not so Great

Frederick the Great, King of Prussia, was not
so great, sultry and sensitive when young, he
wrote bad poetry, refused to bathe, mixed
coffee with champagne, and occasionally wore
rouge, after his father imprisoned him, and had
his lover beheaded outside his window, he
emerged devoted to strict Prussian discipline,

in 1740 he became king and launched his army,
adding a third of Poland and all West Prussia
and Silesia to his domain—to prepare them
for battle, he ordered his officers to take
laxatives and enemas, and, when he found one
officer writing a letter to his wife after curfew,
ordered him to add a final line: "Tomorrow I shall

perish on the scaffold"—Frederick's considered
an enlightened despot, he favored Voltaire
until Voltaire criticized his poetry, yet he declared
serfs and Jews "useless to the state"—impotent,
probably syphilitic, he despised his wife, and when
he died, at his request, was buried with his pet dogs.

# V. Be Sure You're Right

# Hell, According to Jonathan Edwards

Their heads, their eyes, their tongues,
their hands and feet and loins, their
vitals shall forever be full of glowing
melting fire, fierce enough to melt
the very rocks and elements, and also
shall eternally be full of the most quick
and lively sense to feel the torment. . . .
They shall know that they shall never
cease restlessly to plunge and roll
in that mighty ocean of fire.  They will
know that those billows of fire,
that are greater than the highest waves,
will never cease to roll over them,
one following another, forever and ever.

# Mamachtaga's Smile

*"The Indian ascended a ladder placed to the cross timber of the gibbet; and the rope was fastened. When he was swung off, the rope broke and the Indian fell, and having swooned a little, he rose with a smile and went up again."*

--"The Trial of Mamachtaga" (1785), Hugh Henry Brackenridge

In 1785 Mamachtaga, a Delaware warrior
recently returned from the war, was hung
for killing two white men and wounding two
others with a knife, a sad, sudden drunken
assault, "it would appear that the Indian
had been in liquor," Mamachtaga, whose
name—trees blown down by the wind—

signified turbulence and violence, "had been
at war against the settlements" and lately had
camped on Killbuck's Island with the friendly
Lenni Lenape under the protective guns of Fort Pitt,
the fort the new nation's "verge of settlement,"
later the "white men who escaped" claimed
Mamachtaga "without the least notice, rushed

in" and attacked them, Hugh Henry Brackenridge
wrote the narrative, racist yet compassionate,
he a lawyer, judge, writer, publisher, preacher,
poet, and one-time politician, a circuit judge known
for riding naked in rainstorms to keep his clothes
dry, and who in a previous atrocity text atrociously
referred to indigenous people as "animals vulgarly

called Indians"—Brackenridge had loaned one
of the murdered men a blanket that afternoon,
and the next morning rowed over to the island
and discovered Mamachtaga, "now sober," sitting
impassively on a log, claiming he could not recall
what happened the night before, "struck with
the pleasantry of having an Indian for a client,"

Brackenridge, through an interpreter, negotiated
to defend him for a "hundred weight" of beaver,
and Mamachtaga signed a hastily-scrawled contract,
his "mark something like a turkey's foot"—Fort Pitt
having no jail, he was confined in the "black hole,"
a deep pit covered with a heavy door, where
"delinquent or refractory soldiery" were

disciplined, standing above with the interpreter,
Brackenridge conferred with his client yet realized
Mamachtaga misinterpreted the interpreted words
and thought he was trading skins for life, seeing
"the dark and squalid creature" with only a loin cloth
and shirt he declared "humanity dictated" mercy,
and traded away his fee for "a blanket and food

additional to the bread and water"—the white settlers,
hearing that he would defend Mamachtaga, and fearing
he might get him "acquitted by the *crooks of the law*,"
caused a "great noise," and soon a furious mob
gathered before the gate demanding "the surrender
of the Indian," but the fort's commanding officer
"remonstrated and prevailed with them to leave

the Indian to the civil authorities," craving a death,
the mob then resolved to hang the interpreter (who
fled for his life) and force Brackenridge to swear "not
to appear on behalf of the Indian," a freethinker and free
spirit, he refused to yield "to the popular impression,"
and appeared in court to defend when there was

no defense—though "a great warrior," Mamachtaga's
hanging "would not be much regretted"—he "was
a bad man" . . . mischievous in liquor, having killed
two of his own people"—the trial was packed
with misinterpretations, when asked to plead his
innocence or guilt, Mamachtaga was "unwilling
to deny, as unbecoming of a warrior to deny

the truth," declaring only that "he was drunk,"
when "opening his defense," Brackenridge stated
his client "was in liquor, and that this had been
given to him by the white people, the traders
in town," his defense "was overruled" and the jury

"gave their verdict, guilty, without leaving the bar,"
when asked "why sentence of death should not be

pronounced upon him," the question "interpreted
to him," Mamachtaga replied "that he would rather
run awhile," to collect "a gun, horse, fur and the like"
to trade for his life, as he was led away, he was asked
who the judges were, two stern white men in scarlet
robes, and having been among Moravian missionaries,
"he answered that the one, meaning the chief justice,

was God, and the other Jesus Christ"—before his hanging,
Mamachtaga twice had chance to "run awhile—" when
the jailer's child "had taken sick," he offered to cure
her if he could gather "roots from the woods," the jailor,
"taking off his irons . . . let him go to the woods," where
he gathered the medicinals and used them to "cure
the child—" then again, on the morning of the execution,"

Mamachtaga "expressed a wish to be painted that he
might die like a warrior," the jailor "as before unironed
him and took him to the woods to collect his usual paints,"
Brackenridge noted that, "if the Indian had . . . gone
off from the jailor while he was looking for the roots
for the cure or for painting it would have been easy
for him to have made his escape," but Mamachtaga,

having promised to return, did not believe "he had
the physical power to go"—as his execution drew near
"a great body of people assembled" to witness the ritualized
death drama—yet the spectacle requires interpretation—
death did not go as planned—"When he was swung off,
the rope broke and the Indian fell, and having swooned
a little, he rose with a smile and went up again," two ropes

were then "put around his neck," and he "underwent
the sentence of the law, and was hanged till he was
dead." But why did he smile? What were his thoughts?
Was he astonished to still be alive? Was he apologetic for not
dying? Wondering if it was intended? Wondering if he
might yet again run awhile? Or did he think how stupid
white people were, who could not properly kill a warrior?

# "Be Sure You're Right Then Go Ahead": David Not Davy Crockett

Life made him legendary, but death made him immortal,
America's first celebrity, a man famous for being famous,
wildly popular for being wild, for being an unpolished,
uncouth, uneducated, unapologetic frontiersman turned
politician, he happily performed the parts people expected,
imitating his imitations, willingly a caricature, a self-parody,
—myths submerged man—he killed a bear when he was

only 3, he killed 105 bears in 7 months, and one with a knife
at night, he grinned racoons out of trees to save powder, he
straddled a streak of lightning across the sky, he rode his pet
alligator up Niagara Falls, he waded the Mississippi, he caught
the tail of Halley's comet, he could outfight, outhunt, outshoot,
outride, and outtalk any man or woman, all stuff of tall tales—
a New World Hercules enshrined in the American pantheon—

emerging from the dense canebrakes of Tennessee he was
ridiculed as "the gentleman from the cane," when describing
America's experiment with democracy, Alexis de Tocqueville,
was stunned to learn he had been elected: "the inhabitants
of the district . . . sent to the House of Representatives
in Congress an individual . . . who has no education, can
read with difficulty, has no property, no fixed residence,

but passes his life hunting, selling his game to live,
and dwelling continuously in the woods"— he embraced
his role, a homespun man of the people, though he didn't
like to be called Davy—he dressed like a gentleman,
a country squire, and he didn't wear coonskin caps,
though scores of illustrations depicted him wearing one,
he was feted and toasted for his rough western manners,

his life magnified made good filler for eastern newspapers,
but it was an actor's get-rich scheme that made him truly
legendary—*The Lion of the West*, a melodramatic farce
of American innocence and English arrogance, featured
an illiterate but goodhearted frontier congressman, who
strutted onstage wearing a dead opossum for a hat
and announced—"My name is Nimrod Wildfire—half

horse, half alligator and a touch of airthquake—that's
got the prettiest sister, fastest horse, and ugliest dog
in the District, and can outrun, outkick, outjump,
knockdown, drag out, and whip any man in all Kaintuck,"
audiences went wild, the backwoods boasting, the bold
swagger, the confrontations with Mrs. Wollope, a haughty
Englishwoman who disdained Americans—men, women,

and children alike—as being crude, coarse, ignorant
ill-mannered tobacco chewers—everyone took him
for Nimrod—he was at first not amused, but the Lion's
popularity made him a marketable subject, and spurious
memoirs began appearing, fabulous fables of grinning
racoons and riding lightning bolts, he loved and hated
the fabrications and in response marketed his own brand,

publishing his *Narrative*: "obscure as I am, my name is
making a considerable deal of fuss in the world. I can't tell
why it is . . . Go where I will, everybody seems anxious
to get a peep at me,"—he didn't mind the peeping—yet
he lost his next election for opposing Andrew Jackson's
Indian Removal Act—too honest to be a politician, his
reaction was fateful: "I told the people of my District that I

would serve them faithfully . . . but if not, they might go
to hell, and I will go to Texas," and he went, and his death
gave him eternal life, the humorous *Crockett Almanacs*
were peddled for decades, most with illustrations of him
wearing coonskin caps—more than a century later Disney
launched the Crockett Craze, Davy, Davy Crockett,
King of the Wild Frontier, a staged event when television

first began to reach mass audiences, children went wild
for Crockett paraphernalia, faux coonskin caps, faux
fringed deerskin jackets, toy muskets and hatchets, books
and comic books—millions were made during the craze,
the mid-fifties needed American icons, and for a time he
was more popular than either Elvis or Eisenhower, John
Wayne would have preferred to play Sam Houston, but

the money people demanded he put on the coonskin cap,
in the film's death scene, wounded by a lance, he blows up
the powder magazine, another fabulous story—in the 60s
the Crockett Death Wars erupted, did he die swinging Old

Betsy surrounded by a heap of dead Mexicans, or as a captive
bayoneted on his knees, there's even a story of a Mexican salt
mine, the battle for narrative continues, part of a greater war

for the ownership of history, the polemics of possession,
to venerate sacred stories or tear down false idols, but—
long before all the hoopla—he had a simple motto: "Be
sure you're right, then go ahead," and go ahead he did,
his *Narrative* concluded: "I am at liberty to vote as my
conscience and judgment dictates to be right . . . look
at my arms, you will find no handcuffs on them."

# Novel Reading, A Cause of Female Depravity: Lines Taken from *The Monthly Mirror*, November 1797

*Polluted streams again are pure,*
*And deepest wounds admit a cure;*
*But woman no redemption knows—*
*The wounds of honour never close!*
*Pity may mourn, but not restore—*
*And woman falls to rise no more.*

I now begin to hope I shall see good old days come
round again . . . [when] chastity—pure and spotless
CHASTITY!—will once more be the darling attribute

of women. . . . to trace to its source this great calamity . . .
I find those who made novel-reading an indispensable
branch in forming the minds of young women, have

a great deal to answer for. Without this poison . . .
females . . . would never have been so much slaves
of vice. . . . A girl with her intellectual powers enervated

by such . . . reading, falls easy prey to the first boy
who assumes the languishing lover. He has only to stuff
a piece of dirty paper into the crevice of her window,

full of *thous* and *thees* and *thys* . . . and Miss is not long
in finding out that "many waters cannot quench love" . . .
And yet this, bad as it is, is not the worst result of such

pernicious reading. It is no uncommon thing for a young
lady . . . to fix her affections on her dearest friend's
husband, and by artful blandishments allure him

to herself. Be not staggered, moral reader, at the recital!
Such serpents are really in existence. "And was novel-
reading the cause of this?" inquires some gentle fair one. . .

"was novel reading the foundation of such frail conduct?"
I answer yes! It is the school where the poor deluded female

imbibes erroneous principles, and from thence pursues

a flagrantly vicious line of conduct; it is there she is told that love is involuntary, and that attachments of the heart are decreed by fate. Impious reasoning.

# "The Poison They Infuse": Lines Taken from "The Ladies Department" in the *Zion's Herald*, December, 1825

Of all the various evils that corrupt the female mind
in the present day . . . none are more injurious than novel
reading, where it is indiscriminately indulged.  The morality

to which novels and romances often pretend, only serves
to disguise the poison they infuse, and excite a fatal
degree of pride and self-complacency while the pathetic

*tales* and *elegant distresses* with which they often abound . . .
tend to steel the heart against those scenes of misery
which we daily see, and which it is our duty to commiserate

and relieve. . . . No sooner does the young person imbibe
this fatal poison, than she immediately discovers herself
to be unhappy!  Her daily employments—her accustomed

pursuits and associates are no longer capable of pleasing
or interesting . . . her relatives and friends who have never
been so unfortunate as to be introduced to these ideal

scenes of bliss, become irksome and insipid . . . she sighs
to meet some kindred spirit who can share the feelings
of her heart.  She is now prepared for the specious but

designing wiles of the seducer, and happy if her unsuspicious
youth and infatuated ideas do not plunge her in ruin's murky
pit. But allowing her to escape this snare . . . the blissful scene

that fancy painted . . . can never be realized . . . The common
and vulgar cares of life will intrude . . . and thus terminate
the Elysian dreams of life with disgust and unhappiness.

# "The Good Wife": Lines Taken from *The Dawn*, May, 1822

The good wife is . . . ever mindful the solemn contract which she has entered into, is strictly and conscientiously virtuous, constant, and faithful to her husband; chaste, pure, and unblemished in every thought, word, and deed; she is humble and modest, from reason

and conviction; submissive from choice, and obedient from inclination; what she acquires by love and tenderness, she preserves by prudence and discretion; she makes it her business to serve, and her pleasure to oblige her husband; conscious that everything which promotes his

happiness, must in the end contribute to her own: her tenderness relieves his cares, her affection softens his distress, her good humour and complacency lessen and subdue his affliction . . . . Lastly, as a good and pious Christian, she looks up with an eye of gratitude to the great

dispenser and disposer of all things . . . entreating his divine favor . . . this and every other moral and religious duty; well satisfied, that if she duly and punctually discharges her several offices . . . in this life, she shall be blessed and rewarded for it in another.

# "To Rob Sweet Innocence of Its All": Lines Taken from *The Ladies' Visitor*, February, 1820

There is no crime to be deprecated and abhorred as Seduction; yet . . . it is
the only crime of a gross nature that is passed over with levity . . . He who
is guilty of it is permitted to show his brazen face in society, and is frequently

as much respected as those who would shudder at the idea of depriving
the loveliest of Heaven's works of its dearest jewel, Virtue. In the present
age it has become common, nay, I venture to say, *Fashionable*—and it may

be classed with the many vices which Dandyism and Dissipation have
rendered ordinary and consequently *popular*; for no measure is taken
by the proper authorities, to inflict a punishment adequate to the crime,

on those who basely tear the only hope, the only prize, from the breast
of unsuspecting innocence, and leave the lovely victim of their infernal arts,
covered with infamy and shame, to face the bitter criminations of an unfeeling

and censorious world . . . how depraved—how callous—how opposite to all
that is generous, humane and feeling, must be that man, who would court
the affections of lovely woman only to trifle with them! But how much more

depraved—how unlike a man, and how like a demon, is he who will gain the
love of innocent beauty—who will profess eternal attachment—who will swear
by all that is sacred that he adores the object who he addresses—and when he

has . . . disarmed her of all doubts and fears . . . in an evil moment throws
off the blandishments of feigned love stoops to the basest artifice, and rushes,
like a deceitful crocodile, upon his prey; deprives it of all that was dear,

then leaves his helpless victim to pine away in sorrow and despair,
and into an untimely grave, neglected and unwept. Alas! how painful
to every humane and sympathetic mind is the reflection!—The loveliest

flower of nature, that bloomed so fresh and fair . . . is snatched by the ruthless
hand of the Seducer and dashed withering to the earth, faded and dying,
to be the sport of all the pestilential blasts of calumny! . . . The Seducer

comes . . . with professions of love and devotion, to rob sweet innocence
of its all! He comes . . . armed with Hell's impudence . . . without a blush,
without a sorrow—exulting in his accursed conquest!—Oh! If there be a hell—

and that there is we surely dare not doubt . . . the hottest hell, the sharpest woe, will be the base Seducer's merited reward! He is the murderer of Innocence—the robber of Virtue—and the detractor of Perfection!

## Make Belief, The Great American Invention

*"It is not the worst thing that can be said of a country that it gives birth to the confidence man. . . . it is a good thing. . . . that men can be swindled."*
 —Every Duyckinck, *The Literary World*, August 1849

*"Truth uncompromisingly told will always have its ragged edges."*
 —Herman Melville, *Billy Budd, Sailor*, 1886

Flannel's a soft piece of cloth, but it can
also refer to using a lot of words to avoid
telling the truth—originally an animal's
thick fur, fleece can also mean taking
someone's money dishonestly—gulls are

everywhere where there's water, but a gull
is also someone easily tricked or cheated—
rooks are also birds, or a chess piece, but
it's also a verb for swindling and cheating—
mark has many meanings, from the Bible

to visible impressions, symbols, and stains,
but, like gull, it's also a gullible person who's
easy to deceive—bamboozle, to trick or cheat
someone, and grift, to gain money or property
llicitly, are known but rarely heard—then there's

diddling, to deceive the unwary with spurious,
promises, also rarely heard, the first diddler was
Jeremy Diddler, an 1803 farcical character who
constantly borrowed but never repayed, in 1840
Poe published a curious sketch rarely read today,

"Diddling, Considered As One of the Exact Sciences,"
and until a luckless swindler, William Thompson,
 stumbled into a new idiom as he was carried
off to the Tombs, diddling was the popular term
for swindling—there's always been special slang

for hustlers, predicates of pretending—to stiff, sting,
shaft, swizzle, dupe, milk, bilk, snooker, hornswoggle,
hoodwink, and flimflam—but Thompson prompted
a new vernacular—on the streets of New York, he
approached upper-class marks, he equally well

dressed and genteel, and posing as an acquaintance, he
he warmly greeted his targets, after a friendly exchange
to allay suspicions, he asked if they would trust him
with their watch or money—"have you confidence in me
to trust me with your watch until to-morrow"—to avoid

awkwardness of not remembering someone, his targets
often acquiesced—he worked his scam until July, 1849,
when a previous victim, swindled out of a gold watch,
saw him on the street and had him arrested—a *New York
Herald* reporter satirically referred to him as the "Confidence

Man," a month later *The National Police Gazette*, known
popularly as the barbershop bible, described the diddle
as a "confidence game,"—damned by dollars much of his
life, Melville symbolically published his ninth novel on April
Fool's Day, 1857, *The Confidence-Man: His Masquerade*,

a dense text of emblems and allegories, of shadows
and shades, where what's seen is mostly unseen, where
scores of travelers embark—again symbolically on April
Fool's Day—on a Mississippi steamboat, both characters
and readers are pressed to assess the claims of strangers

in an uncertain world of unstable truths and verities,
—sales were poor and reviewers unkind, but the term
stuck, and shopkeepers began putting up signs, "No
Trust,"—America's a land of opportunity, a land
of make believe, of making belief, where identity's

performed, truth's transacted, and perception's
manipulated, where self-interest's universal and self-
creation profitable—confidence men, self-made men
without substance or conscience, peddle promises,
and confidence games promote acts of faithless faith.

To paraphrase a prophet:

the manipulation of belief
makes behavior foolish,
always better to distrust
than risk becoming brutish.

## Victor "The Count" Lustig, The Smoothest Con Man that Ever Lived

*"Everything turns gray when I don't have at least one mark on the horizon. Life seems empty and depressing. I cannot understand honest men. They lead desperate lives, full of boredom."*
  —Victor "The Count," Lustig

Supposedly, he was 57 when he died, but much of his life was supposedly, his death certificate identified him as Robert V. Miller, one of countless aliases, and listed his occupation as "apprentice salesman," a joke—he was unquestionably one

of the world's greatest salesmen, the man who sold the Eiffel Tower—twice, Victor "The Count" Lustig, variously labeled as "America's most dangerous con man," "history's most daring—and flamboyant—con man," "the smoothest con man that ever lived," and

"the Heavyweight Champion of the Art of the Swindle"; a life fabricated in fiction and deception, he was "as elusive as a puff of cigarette smoke and as charming as a young girl's dream," constantly shifting stages, scenes, and schemes, he was everyone but no one,

his most notorious artifice was selling the Eiffel Tower— posing as a corrupt French official, and carrying forged documents, he wined and dined a group of scrap metal dealers, informing them that, due to disrepair, maintenance costs, and post-war expenses, the Eiffel

Tower was for sale, bidding would be secret and bribes required; one eager buyer paid around 70,000 francs, over $7 million—flush with funds, Lustig fled to Austria and scanned newspapers for stories of his con, but none appeared, his mark too embarassed to inform

the police, after a few months he returned to Paris, once again offering to sell the Eiffel Tower, but Parisian police were informed, and he escaped to the states—

a lifelong grifter, he, supposedly, was born in 1890
in a small Austria-Hungarian village, his parents

variously either genteel or the "poorest peasant people,"
he began as a street hustler, pickpocket, burglar,
and gambler, according to *True Detective Mysteries*, he
perfected card tricks until he could make cards "do
everything but talk," charming and cultivated, fluent

in five languages, he made frequent voyages across
the Atlantic fleecing first-class passengers while posing
as a Broadway producer, stockbroker, and/or investor,
when WW I ended ocean travel, he toured the states,
and became notorious as a smooth-talking swindler

in 40 different cities, his marks variously described him
as a "dear friend," and "as warm and sincere a human being
as they knew," his favorite ruse was the Romanian Money
Box, a seemingly miraculous contrivance of mahogany
and brass the size of a steamer trunk, a Jazz Age ATM

fueled by radium, the new miracle science, it, as it appeared,
printed crisp $100 bills—eager to get rich quick, marks across
the US paid thousands to possess it, including a Texas sheriff,
who, incensed at the fraud, chased Lustig back to Chicago, but
the no-account Count conned him into believing he had used

the box incorrectly, and as a gesture of good faith, he paid
the peacekeeper compensation in counterfeit bills for his
trouble—an inevitable evolution, Lustig determined making
money was the easiest way to make money. and during
the Depression his $100 bills were "so flawless they fooled

even bank tellers," using a nationwide string of carriers
to pass his make-believe money, he dispersed thousands
of dollars each month for five years, so much that one
judge declared the enterprise was "like some government,
issuing money in rivalry with the United States Treasury,"

—jealousy, not greed, brought him down, learning
that Lustig was pursuing a younger woman, his mistress,
a madam who managed a brothel, tipped the police,
and he was arrested in New York, and a key secreted
in a pocket led to a Times Square subway locker containing

$51,000 in spurious bills and the engraving plates, yet
the day before his trial the world's "greatest con-man"
escaped from—supposedly—the inescapable Federal
House of Detention, having fashioned a rope of bed
sheets, he slipped out a window and when spotted

on the street, pretended he was washing windows—
months later, after a car chase, he was again arrested,
when surrounded by guns, he calmly said, "Well, boys,
here I am," another joke, since being was never being there,
he was a fabulist, a story seller constantly selling stories

so intricate they will never be unraveled, he was never
who he said he was, and even his jailhouse interviews,
supposedly to set right a life of lies, fabricated further
untruths, research has yet to discover who he was—
perhaps he never was, "there is not a scrap of evidence

that Lustig was ever born," a lifetime of lies left no self
behind the self, a sleight-of-hand life of misdirection,
of supposing and assuming, left nothing behind the masks
and masquerades, yet whoever he was, he was an American
exemplar of making something of nothing, of making belief.

# If You Believe This . . . George C. Parker and the Brooklyn Bridge

*Wikipedia* calls him "one of the most successful con men
in the history of the United States, as well as one history's most
talented hoaxers," George C. Parker, who sold the Brooklyn
Bridge to unwary immigrants countless times, sources disagree
but generally agree he sold and resold the bridge for decades—

preferring fables, some sites state he sold the bridge twice
a week for thirty years, or forty years—a polished performer,
clever and convincing, Parker preyed on the most vulnerable,
immigrants literally as they stepped off the boat from Ellis Island—
staging a well-rehearsed routine, Parker deftly deceived—

the posh suit, the smooth talk, the forged deeds, the fake office
the bogus "For Sale" sign tacked to bridge—America, land
of opportunity, performances without substance—they were
blinded by dazzle and glare, by promises of prosperity, desperate
yearnings for a new life—Parker touched his targets for $50

to $50,000, and many never knew they were duped until they
started building tolls booths—indifferent to worthless deeds
of sale, piteous pleas and panic, and shattered dreams, police
removed the barriers and victims—welcome to America, land
of the opportunistic—Parker was so successful selling the bridge

that he sold other public properties, the Metropolitan Museum
of Art, Madison Square Garden, Grant's Tomb, and the Statue
of Liberty, that shining torch to the golden door, that beacon
to the huddled masses—he lied for a living, but several times
Parker was arrested, for larceny, forgery, and impersonating

a police officer, and once he escaped by donning a sheriff's
hat and coat and walking out of the courthouse, such a slick
operator—in 1928, after his fourth and final arrest, he received
mandatory life in Sing Sing—yet a celebrity in prison, he enjoyed
his forced retirement, enjoyed entertaining guards and inmates

with stories of his scams, renditions of predatory performances,
recitals of betrayed trust, his audiences laughed at the plight

of nameless others, foreigners learning a valuable lesson, America, land of fleece and flimflam, of ends justifying means, where faithless audacity is celebrated and victims of deception are forgotten.

# The White Slavery Conspiracy: "The Greatest Crime In The World's History"

*"These murderous traffickers drink the heart's blood of weeping mothers while they eat the flesh of their daughters."*
  —Fighting The Traffic In Young Girls, Or War on the
    White Slave Trade, 1910

During the first decade of the twentieth century it was called—repeatedly—"The Greatest Crime In The World's History," "The greatest shame and sin of our civilization," and "the blackest slavery that has ever stained the human race," White Slavery, "this hideous monster . . . this curse

of humanity," thousands of people were in outraged panic, believing "*Thousands Upon Thousands of Young Girls* are annually sold into a life of sin . . . *Young girls from 13 to 20* are *daily* being *stolen* and *sold* into houses of ill fame," thoroughly racist, repugnant, and repulsive, such frantic, feverish belief

in a world-wide conspiracy commanding devilish hordes "whose sole business is luring young girls away from home and selling them to keepers of dives to live a life that is worse than death," pimps and procurers, "these hell-hounds who make a business of dealing in young girls," were everywhere,

a sinister syndicate of fiends kidnapping, drugging, and smuggling young girls, even an "ordinary ice cream parlor is very likely to be a spider's web," train stations, theaters, restaurants, candy stores, amusement parks—"All over these places Satan has his agents stationed," and dance halls, "truly the ante-room of Hell itself,"

snared scores of girls. Emigrants and foreigners were blamed: "Many of these white slave traders are recruited from the scum of Europe," in 1907 *McClure's Magazine* intoned the traffickers were "largely composed of Russian Jews," and to combat this wrecking of American female innocence— "the worst doom

that can befall a woman," an army of vice commissions and vigilance associations was enlisted in hundreds of cities and towns, recruiting thousands of indignant Americans to wage

"a holy crusade against the vice of men who would . . . besmirch
the purity of womanhood," these the most misguided reformers

of the not-so Progressive Era. But where did it all come from,
this hysterical terror of nonnatives stealing and ruining young
white girls, this panicked manic of othering? What spawns
such sightless, insidious bias over such vast expanses of time
and space? Witch hunts erupt during times of pandemic change

when what was becomes lost in waves of transition, when what
used to be no longer is, and when insecure people seek to blame.
Such was America when, not pimps and procurers, but the bright
lights of cities lured young people away from their rural homes,
their new urban environments offering unprecedented freedoms,

family-centered systems of supervision fell apart, young women
living and working alone provoked the worst fears imaginable,
fed by terrors of unfettered emigration, nefarious conspiracies
perceiving heartless demons circling tenements and factories,
morality in decline. Muckraking journalists and unscrupulous

politicians fueled the fires, their rampant rhetoric depicting dark
visions of evil unrestrained, hundreds of newspapers, magazines,
pamphlets, and books disseminated sensationalized stories
of innocent girls abducted by heartless foreigners, politicians
campaigned on promises to make America pure again, in 1910

the panic peaked with the publication of *Fighting The Traffic
in Young Girls, Or War On The White Slave Trade*, a national
bestseller, and with Congress passing the "White-Slave Traffic
Act," which made it a federal crime to transport "any woman
or girl for the purpose of prostitution, or debauchery, or for

any other immoral purpose," a botched law primarily used
to prosecute premarital and extramarital sex, and mixed-
race relationships—the national fetish (innocent girls living
a life worse than death) was soon sucked into a new national
hysteria—a world war with the Kaiser and the Dirty Huns.

# VI. Epilogue: Great Values On Prehistoric Artifacts

# A Weird Word, Wild: How the Natural Became Unnatural

A weird word, wild,
definitions abound,
yet distort the real,
the raw, the natural,
nature's not uninhabited,
uncultivated, or primitive,
nor uncivilized, savage, or
inhospitable, nor crazed,
distracted, or rabid,
nor harsh, barbarous, or
violent, nor feral, brutish,
or turbulent, nor tangled,
distraught, or frantic,
nor desolate, furious, or
vicious, nor daft, reckless,
or random, simply nature
is that which remains
beyond human touch,
that which remains
unmarked and unspoiled.

# Archaeopteryx, The Feathered Lizard

A missing link not altogether missing, a bird-like
dinosaur, its name means old wing, a transitional
creature the Archaeopteryx, a non-avian feathered
lizard, popularly the oldest bird yet not a bird,

this first bird lived in the late Jurassic, 150 million
years ago, in Bavaria, then an archipelago of tropical
islands in a shallow sea, about the size of a magpie,
or maybe raven, this feathered bird-lizard had more

in common with Mesozoic dinosaurs than modern
birds, jaws with sharp teeth, three fingers with claws,
a long bony tail, and hyperextensible second toes,
its killing claw, a transitional fossil, its feathers suggest

warm-bloodedness, its discovery, about the time
of Darwin, fueled the evolution dispute, the dinosaur
to bird debate, an argument still being argued among
both scientists and crazies, it displays features

of both, notably well-developed flight feathers, thought
to be matte black, or maybe dark variations, but no
iridescence, there's only a few specimens more or less
full, artifacts of preservation preserved in the death

poses, head, neck, and tail bent downward, suggesting
they dropped and drifted on their backs, floating for
a time, until embedded in anoxic sediment, the greatest
contention among paleobiologists concerns flying,

if the archaeopteryx flew by flapping, or simply glided,
wings and tail suggest lift generation, but the bony
breastbone suggest it was not a strong flier, incapable
of flapping flight, yet its wings were large, its feathers

asymmetrical, unlike flightless birds, interestingly its
brain was significantly larger than most dinosaurs,
its vision capacity taking up one-third of its brain,
not bird-brained at all, some argue the trees-down

hypothesis, that it was a semi-arboreal climbing
animal that glided through the trees, others imagine
it ran along the ground, the ground-up hypothesis,
flight evolving from running, using its wings mainly

to escape predators, glides interspersed with strong
downward strokes, but then perhaps like modern
crows it felt at home both in trees and on ground,
ancient Jurassic Bavaria was more like Florida today,

only drier, and the Archaeopteryx probably lived
among the semi-arid, sub-tropical islands, the shallow
lagoons of a distant world, feeding on smaller lizards,
insects, and the scraps tossed up by the shallow sea,

there are restorations and drawings, but there's still
controversy, and much unknown about this old winged
creature that inhabited the separate realms of earth
and air, that was first discovered by a single feather,

it lived, flapping, gliding, feeding, escaping a world
of tooth and claw, today it feeds imaginations, the grist
of eternal discussions, did it squawk or sing, what did
it see with its splendid eyes, what can it teach about life?

# Tracking Dinosaurs: Darwinism, Creationism, and Capitalism in the Muck of Time

Abstract: There's a story here, convoluted
but clear, of timelines confused, the boasts
of human arrogance, apex predators stalking
prey, dinosaurs and humans, unlearned lessons,
the irony of geology confounded, and signs
lost and found and lost, this way to the egress.

*Part I: Dinosaur Valley State Park*

Around 113 million years ago, early Cretaceous
Period, Glen Rose was a seaside resort, a sultry
tropical climate of giant palm and conifer trees
lining the shores of a shallow sea covering much

of Texas, a watery world of beaches, lagoons,
and coral reefs, the water teeming with curious
creatures, carnivorous marine reptiles, sharks,
bony fish, ammonites and rudists, those large

conical reef-building bivalves, on land dinosaurs
dominated, a temperate ice-free world of dense
forests, where flowering plants first appeared,
 and new species of birds and mammals, at some

point, give or take a few million years, both
sauropods and theropods left their tracks
in the soft limey mud that bordered the sea,
the mud the deposit of billions of shells

over countless eons, the muck hardening
to limestone after millions more years passed,
the tracks remained, buried in sediment until
the Paluxy River flooded a century or so ago,

exposing the three-toed theropod prints, not
long after, while searching for a place to hide
his still, a moonshiner stumbled on the saucer-
shaped sauropod prints, during the Depression

locals made money selling moonshine and
chiseling out fossils and tracks to sell, nearly
a decade later, after discovering a near perfect
theropod track in a New Mexico trading post,

fossil hunter Roland T. Bird visited Glen Rose
to trace the track's origins and was astounded
to find the sauropod prints, announcing the first
sauropod tracks ever found on land, he shook

up the dinosaur world, previous science had
assumed sauropods only inhabited water, their
bodies too huge and too heavy for land travel,
the largest dinosaurs, sauropods were massive

plant-eaters with pillar-like legs and large feet,
perhaps the tracks belong to Sauroposeidon Proteles
a 50-ton sauropod standing 20-feet high and 100-feet
long, its graceful, giraffe-like neck 40-feet long, much

longer than its tail, they traveled in herds, the young
protected in the center with the adults on the outside—
theropods were carnivores, and the Glen Rose tracks
perhaps belong to Acrocanthosaurus, an apex predator,

a high-spined hunting lizard like T-Rex that ran on two
feet while pursuing its prey, perhaps the theropod stalked
the slower-moving sauropod, Roland T. Bird discovered
a long trackway of theropod and sauropod tracks side-

by-side, life and death in the sludge of time—the Dinosaur
Valley State Park opened in 1972, the tracks its main
attraction, near the entrance there's a gift shop and two
life-size dinosaurs, sauropod and theropod, plaster

and fiberglass leftovers first displayed at the 1965 New
York World's Fair, today both look a bit frayed, the park
offers over 20-miles hiking, horse, and bike trails,
woods of juniper, oak, pecan, mesquite, cottonwood,

and sycamore, prairie grass in the open fields, several
scenic overlooks with benches, and perhaps glimpses
of the endangered Golden-Cheek Warbler, the Black-
Capped Vireo, deer, raccoons, turkeys, armadillos,

snakes and lizards are plentiful, and coyotes lurk at night,
on pleasant weekends the park's packed, and near
the tracks bathers cool off in the river, during peak
hours the gift shop's crowded, children rush excitedly

through the shelves and bins seeking dinosaurs, cold
drinks, and ice cream bars, for RVers there's hookups
for overnighting, for their $8 entry fee visitors get a map
of the best tracks, trails, parking, and restroom facilities.

*Part II: The Creation Evidence Museum*

Strategically placed down the road from the park,
there's the Creation Evidence Museum, here there's
a different story, a creation message opposing
evolutionary theory, there's a replica of Noah's

Ark, the culmination of 40 years of research and 18
months of craftsmanship, with a long online exegesis
on how so many creatures, including "some *dinosaurs*,"
were carried so far for so long, there's also a replica

of the Stegosaurus carved on a Cambodian temple
column, the temple dedicated in 1186—a fossilized
human finger dug up in Cretaceous layers near
the Paluxy River, the finger identified as the fourth

finger of a girl's left hand—the London Artifact (London,
TX), a hammer embedded in Cretaceous limestone,
the "artifact unreproducable [sic] by modern scientific
methods," and several Cretaceous Period fossil prints

of human feet alongside dinosaur tracks, proving they
lived side-by-side—in The Burdick Track "all the toes
and arches . . . are clearly discernable [sic]—" another
footprint in rock, The Meister Print, a human sandal

print "with some stitching . . . along the edges" crushes
two trilobites—in the Alvis Delk Cretaceous Footprint
there's two prints together, human and dinosaur—like
a fossilized pictograph, The Hand Print in Stone has

"all five human digits and the palm impression . . . clearly visible" in Cretaceous rock—"wishing to see the truth of creation made known," the museum advertises "Public and Homeschool dinosaur track and human footprint

events," a Dino Discovery Lab, a Biosphere Project "Re-creating What It Was Like Before Noah's Flood," and dozens of Books & DVDs, and Web Cast Videos on YouTube, including the Creation In Symphony series—"It's an experience like no other."


*Part III: Dinosaur World*

Then there's Dinosaur World, an educational family fun experience, located "just around the corner from Dinosaur Valley State Park," on the corner of Park Road and US 67, and visible to all Glen Rose

visitors—there's a giant T-Rex out front—for full admission (Adults $27.95, Kids 3-12 $23.95) visitors can step back in time and "wander among hundreds of life-sized dinosaurs in a natural setting," or relax

in the covered picnic area, "coolers encouraged—bring your own healthy snacks and drinks" while kids play in the "Dino-themed playground," for interactive fun, kids can visit the gemstone mine and pan for real gems

(everyone receives a free Lucky Strike Bag at the Dino Gem Excavation), or kids can take part in The Fossil Dig, "a 15-minute guided activity in a specially stocked pit," where they can dig for shark teeth, gastropods, stingray

barbs, and Mosasaur teeth—"They can select three of their favorites to take home," offering endless fun, kids can also visit the Bone Yard and help "uncover the 27-foot skeleton from under the sand"—"friendly dogs on leashes

are welcome" everywhere except inside the museum and gift shop, where 20 animatronics come to life, and where "great values on prehistoric artifacts as well as toys, games and gorgeous geodes" can be discovered.

## About the Author

Dan Williams is the Director of TCU Press and the TCU Honors Professor of Humanities. He has authored or co-authored a dozen books and over fifty articles, publications which include two novels and two collections of poetry. His first collection of poetry, *Past Purgatory, A Distant Paradise,* was named the 2017 Best Book of Poetry Award by the Philosophical Society of Texas.

www.ingramcontent.com/pod-product-compliance
Lightning Source LLC
Chambersburg PA
CBHW061943220426
43662CB00012B/2013